COMISKEY

NAKED SURRENDER

COMING HOME

TO OUR TRUE

SEXUALITY

IVP Books

An imprint of InterVarsity Press
Downers Grove, Illinois

InterVarsity Press
P.O. Box 1400, Downers Grove, IL 60515-1426
World Wide Web: www.ivpress.com
E-mail: email@ivpress.com

InterVarsity Press® is the book-publishing division of InterVarsity Christian Fellowship/USA®, a
movement of students and faculty active on campus at hundreds of universities, colleges and schools
of nursing in the United States of America, and a member movement of the International Fellowship
of Evangelical Students. For information about local and regional activities, write Public Relations
Dept., InterVarsity Christian Fellowship/USA, 6400 Schroeder Rd., P.O. Box 7895, Madison, WI
53707-7895, or visit the IVCF website at <www.intervarsity.org>.

Design: Cindy Kiple
Images: naked man bending down: Loungepark/Getty Images
        woman's back: Giorgio Fochesato/iStockphoto
        muscular man: dundanim/iStockphoto

ISBN 978-0-8308-3298-9

Printed in the United States of America ∞

Library of Congress Cataloging-in-Publication Data

Comiskey, Andrew.
    Naked surrender: coming home to our true sexuality/Andrew
Comiskey.
        p. cm.
    Includes bibliographical references (p.   ).
    ISBN 978-0-8308-3298-9 (pbk.: alk. paper)
    1. Chastity. 2. Sex—Religious aspects—Christianity. I. Title.
    BV4647.C5C66 2010
    241'.66—dc22

                                                                    2010014320

P	18	17	16	15	14	13	12	11	10	9	8	7	6	5	4	3	2	1
Y	25	24	23	22	21	20	19	18	17	16	15	14	13	12	11	10		

To Mauricio Montion and Maria Cardenas
whose faithful persistence released Aquas Vivas (Living Waters)
throughout Latin America

To Katie Comiskey
whose truthful beauty honors both her heavenly and her
earthly father

To Annette for fruitfulness;
new life springs daily from our life together

Imagine yourself as a living house. God comes in to rebuild the house. At first, perhaps, you can understand what he is doing. He is getting the drains right and stopping the leaks in the roof and so on: you knew that those jobs needed doing and so you are not surprised. But presently he starts knocking the house about in a way that hurts abominably and does not seem to make sense. What on earth is he up to? The explanation is that he is building quite a different house from the one you thought of—throwing out a new wing here, putting on an extra floor there, running up towers, making courtyards. You thought you were going to be made into a decent little cottage: but he is building a palace. He intends to come and live in it himself.

C. S. LEWIS
Mere Christianity (BOOK IV, CH. 9)

CONTENTS

1

AT HOME IN THE BODY

RESTING IN HIS RESCUE

Today salvation has come to this house. . . . For the Son of Man came to seek and to save what was lost.

LUKE 19:9-10

You also, like living stones, are being built together into a spiritual house to be a holy priesthood.

1 PETER 2:5

The news from home back in the United States chilled me. Why did I pick up the newspaper anyway? Headline news— another pastor bites the dust. But this toothy guy was big: he hobnobbed with presidents, championed family values, built a megachurch and headed up the National Association of Evangelicals. And apparently slept with a male prostitute for three years. What a disconnect: serving the house of God with a divided house.

A body in shame. The Body of Christ in shame. The church in the United States, perhaps the richest and most visible in the world, exposed before the world by the very cameras that magnified its good news.

I thought of my friends in the United States and abroad: men and women who love Jesus and want nothing more than to glorify him in their bodies. Who struggle to do so well in light of a bewildering array of mirrors and messages. Signposts in the church and world confuse; these individuals' normal longings for love get submerged or exaggerated. And now the sheep lose another shepherd and maybe find another reason to dismiss the Body as irrelevant to the realities coursing through their own bodies.

I prayed for mercy, for the powerful compassion of Jesus to meet my friends where they feel harassed, even helpless, in light of another's failure. "Tend to your own, O God. Gather them; carry them close to your heart. Raise up men and women to shepherd them wisely and well in these crucial areas of their sexuality and relationships."

I took heart as I flew from Buenos Aires to my next destination, and considered what God had been doing in our midst. Over a couple of weeks, we had gathered in several different cities in South America. I had a little team with me, Jake and Bev, and would meet up with a few new team members in our next city. We were united in our broken histories and in Jesus' ongoing work of "house cleaning and repair." As we made known his mercy in our lives, that same mercy rose like a river to cleanse and restore others. Brave little churches—houses of God—became equipped to release those waters to individual homes—the men and women of God.

Personal weakness was no match for those who came boldly to receive mercy. For many, if not most, it was the first time they had faced sexual matters in the church. They were getting real about their own bodies in the Body.

That has been my call for a while now—going to the nations with the good news of how Jesus meets us through fellow sinners and gives us a realistic way forward to recover "whole-enough" sexuality. (By "whole-enough" sexuality I mean the freedom to cultivate holy desire for the opposite sex, and to work out that desire shoulder to shoulder with same-sex friends.) If the church is serious about this work, then we mentor and train their lay leaders to actually "dig deep wells" of mercy, small discipleship groups called Living Waters; these groups then become that church's pastoral care arm for those in need.

BECOMING WHOLE ENOUGH

Bev and Jake had dug wells of Living Waters with me in North America and now traveled with me a bit. Jake loved giving out of the overflow of God's mercy to him. Having been forgiven of much, he loved much. When I first met Jake, he was a former young-adult leader who had been busted for crossing a lot of lines. The then twenty-two-year-old knew that if Jesus and the Body of Christ could not help him exercise authority over his porn habit and the blurred boundaries with girlfriends, then he could be lost. He was sick of his compromises—sicker of his own than of the double-minded men he had witnessed in his family and church. He knew then that if Jesus did not become his answer, he wanted out of Christian community altogether.

Bev knew these compromises well. Having been sexually abused by her uncle, she sought refuge in Christ but could not find rest in his Body. Her uncle was an elder in her church, and her entire family (who at the time knew nothing about the

abuse) worshiped there too. She left home for university. She
threw herself into her studies and Christian service and tried to
avoid intimacy with others. She grew to trust a similarly
wounded female friend, a friendship that became sexual. It felt
safe and dangerous at the same time. She left the relationship
only to discover another one, then another. Her "house" and
the corporate house of Christ had become a conflict for her,
more a curse than a blessing.

Bev and Jake needed help and began to receive it through
some wise counseling and a group of people who loved them
well for a long time. They began to experience a glimmer of
hope. Could Jesus through his Body really grant them grace to
overcome sin? Did they really want to overcome that sin? Could
he reclaim their bodies as a gift and not a threat? And might
these relationships in the Body sustain them on that road to
whole-enough sexuality?

As I glanced over at the two of them dozing off, I remembered where they had come from and where they were now:
good and trustworthy gifts to others, based on God's limitless
love and an awareness of their own limits, weaknesses that inspire them to truth-telling and the mercy it invites. As a result,
both love imperfectly yet well—clearly and mercifully. They
are whole enough. And they manifest whole-enough sexuality
in their relationships.

That's why I wrote this book—to give hope and handles for
recovering that whole-enough state. It cannot be done in isolation. Whole-enough "houses" require the house of God. We recover together in a beautiful interplay of Jesus' real presence in
the Body imparting to our bodies. We discover that we are that
Body, and invite others into that recovery.

I reflected on the pastor's scandal in the newspaper and what
we had just witnessed through our offering: breakdowns and

prospective breakthroughs, broken bodies seeking wholeness in the broken, being-raised Body.

AUTHORITY AND MERCY

I thought about Jesus' exhortation to Peter that the church would be a rock against which hell would not prevail (Matthew 16:18). I prayed: "Let mercy rise in your house, Jesus, and cast out every robber that has raided your people and made us robbers in our own right. Free us to receive every good gift you have for us, that we might become good gifts to others!"

I meditated on Paul's words to the Corinthians when he exhorted them: "Don't you know that you yourselves are God's temple and that God's Spirit lives in you? If anyone destroys God's temple, God will destroy him; for God's temple is sacred, and you are that temple" (1 Corinthians 3:16-17). Paul was helping the Corinthians to own their authority as the temple, the church. Broken as they were, Paul called them onto something greater and truer; he charged them to own their new birthright as a people of God, to walk in the Spirit who confirms them as God's people, and to do no further damage to their corporate gathering.

That meant something to me. We as Christ's Body impact one another for better and for worse. For better, we can build on the Rock. The consequences "for worse" are grave. We can tear down other bodies in the Body, destruction that incurs God's wrath.

I thought of Jake and the poor example of the men in his life, a generational infidelity he had inherited in his church that he was refusing and overcoming; and Bev suffering at the perverse hands of another then the entrapment of her own poor choices. I thought of Paul's words to the Thessalonians about the injustice of sexual immorality: "In this matter no one should wrong

his brother [or sister] or take advantage of [another]" (1 Thessalonians 4:6). I considered the greater power of God's mercy
and the amazing men and women who had stood with me on
my own journey out of homosexuality and into whole-enough
heterosexuality.

On that plane I felt the presence of that "great cloud of wit-
nesses": men and women who had interceded for me, spoken the
truth in love, prayed insightfully into profound areas of wounded-
ness and need, and simply stood with me for extended periods,
wooing me with the gracious witness of Jesus when I felt more
inclined to my familiar state of exile. I saw a stream of faces.

I beheld Jesus who had met me mercifully through his Body.
I recounted the psalmist's sober gratitude when he said: "The
LORD works righteousness and justice for all the oppressed"
(Psalm 103:6). That justice and righteousness came through
Christ, revealed in a variety of men and women. I glimpsed a
mosaic of Christ composed of many faces, faithful ones who
did their part in the redemption of this life. I needed to be reminded because I felt weak. Weary in doing well, I had no natural power to generate faith for the next advance at hand.

God helped me through sweet recollections of his body.

FACING WARFARE

We landed on the outskirts of Santa Cruz, the largest city in
Bolivia. Our view was obscured by a swirling blanket of smoke.
Not a good start, I thought. A fellow passenger told me that this
was the burning season, a weeklong period in which farmers
surrounding the city burn their fields. The city seemed to be
choking under a low ceiling of hot ash and soot.

I was also told that this was Independence Weekend, an extended four-day celebration of that nation's freedom from Span-
ish rule. From the haze I could see revelers gearing up on the

city streets. And in the hotel, I noticed shiny, sexy people primed and ready for action in the big town.

Not helpful. Their example encouraged my worst impulses. A busload of Europeans landed and began to cavort in the hotel pool, wearing poor excuses for clothing. (I think sheer nudity would have been less provocative.) I considered how to stay clean in my thoughts. I know that immorality begins quietly, in the heart, but pride prevented me from making noise about it. I could call my amazing wife Annette back in the States, but why bother her with more than just the burden imposed by my absence? I could also tell either of my trusted teammates, but I chose not to. I was the leader of this advance, grand purveyor of purity and order. Big guys don't tell.

So I approached the battle on my own. I started well enough, in Scripture: I recalled Paul's words: "'Everything is permissible for me'—but not everything is beneficial. 'Everything is permissible for me'—but I will not be mastered by anything" (1 Corinthians 6:12). I think he was referring to the Corinthian's tolerance of sexual immorality; they tended toward a kind of cheap grace, emphasizing a divine love that covers a multitude of sins but does not require saints to forsake those sins.

Paul makes a great point and one that I could grasp in light of my peculiar circumstance. Yes, God's grace is sufficient but should not that grace be activated somehow to stop me from sinning—be it in thought (extended fantasy, transferring that fantasy onto others) or deed (in my case, masturbation)? In light of my call to be faithful to Annette and to those I was called to serve in that city, it was hardly beneficial for me to get lost in the fog of my own fantasyland.

At the very least, such unrealities dulled me to God's greater purposes for others in the land: I had to think of those who were looking to the team and me for help, not just what seemed pleasant to me. And I had to think of Annette. I made a vow of faithfulness to her when we married. We sealed that pledge with our bodies. Paul says later to the Corinthians that husbands and wives give the other authority over their bodies when they marry (1 Corinthians 7:3).

In other words, don't withhold from your spouse. To entertain other lovers in my mind was a kind of withholding from her. And that entertainment could readily master me and become compulsive, even as Paul challenged the Corinthians. I just had to admit that I was weak and weary. I wanted my wife. I had been away from her for two weeks. That day it seemed two weeks too many. Without her, I felt subject to the sexy happenings in that smoky town.

But I still would not tell.

I had yet to get real with how spiritually deadening my immoral musings were. Once again, Paul helped. I reread Paul's rather mysterious line in 1 Corinthians 6:13 when he said: "'Food for the stomach and the stomach for food'—but God will destroy them both. The body is not meant for sexual immorality, but for the Lord, and the Lord for the body." Paul was referencing another Corinthian distortion. They were influenced by a kind of dualism, a split between body and Spirit. For them, even immoral sex was a natural function like eating; it could thus exist on a track separate from the spiritual life without disturbing it!

Paul was adamant: God cares about what goes on in the temple. He created the body and sexuality for holy purposes. His destiny for humanity involves our bodies! Far from being disinterested in them, he cares about our individual temples with the eye of an architect and the strength of a guard. Simply put, God cares about the body, its passions and what we do with them. Those who tend to deny that reality, as did the

Corinthians, damage their spiritual relationship with God. What we do with our bodies matters to him. We are his and that means engaging with him meaningfully at the level of our longings for others.

Struggling alone in a smoky, sexy land, I determined that I wanted the Lord. I did not want to grieve him and his Spirit by hiding away in my illusions. Yes, I wanted to fulfill the mission at hand; I wanted to do it well. And yes, I wanted to remain true to Annette. But more than anything, I wanted Jesus. Without being true to him, I was sunk.

Bev and Jake had gone out with our hosts for a late night meal. Alone in the room, still struggling and agitated, I discovered to my dismay and intrigue that the hotel offered free porn on TV. That was a familiar trap for me—the main reason I prefer roommates in places that tend to offer the filth. After even a few frames of writhing and moaning I knew I could be utterly lost. It made explicit all the thinly veiled temptations of the day. I knew the drug-like power of porn: its promises of beauty and sensual adventure, as well as a type of self nurture for the weary and lonely.

As well, I knew my historic habits and the fragility of my sobriety. I knew that the darkness streaming into my house would do lasting damage to the temple; porn had power to sear indelible images upon its walls that could harass me for years unless I took decisive action. Somehow, by God's grace, I raced from the porn scene, recalling Paul's exhortation to "flee fornication." I have learned not to dialogue with familiar demons. I waited in the hotel lobby for the team and in the meantime phoned Annette.

That was my first connection with another in my struggle. Talking to Annette was like talking with Jesus; it activated the words of Scripture like nothing else could. She learned long ago not to personalize my struggles but rather to stand with me in my weakness as to prevent it from becoming wickedness.

We agreed together: "This body is not meant for sexual immorality but for the Lord." No longer alone in my struggle and sin, I welcomed the grace that poured from her like clean water from a fountain. The presence of another Christian freed me to realize that I did not want foul and false things. I wanted Jesus. And he gave himself freely and tangibly through his body, beginning with my lovely wife.

But to do God's will I needed more than a phone call. I needed Jesus in his body, right there in a faraway land. The factors that made me vulnerable in the first place still remained: weariness, a seductive environment, my own yearning for connection that Annette could not satisfy from afar, as well as a significant spiritual advance at hand which probably invited demonic attack.

Why demonic attack against a little insignificant band of recovering Christians? The enemy of our souls is proud. He hates it when saints gather to humble themselves and confess their desperation for Jesus Christ. And the devil hates what God raises up from our humble gatherings: the very image of God in humanity—men and women learning to dignify each other through pure and earthy blessing of each other. Satan hates God's image in us and will pull out all the stops to bar us from gathering. He seems to particularly enjoy preying upon our weaknesses in order to isolate and condemn us. God turns that around and makes our weaknesses the very ground for mercy and fresh advances of genuine community life.

BECOMING GOD'S HOUSE

This particular advance involved several different types of gathering, including a three-day conference in a church. Over the course of those days, we had gathered a core team to intercede

and prayerfully minister to others. We pledged to faithfully uphold one another in these days, to "submit to one another out of
reverence for Christ" (Ephesians 5:21). We covenanted to become fellow priests who would mutually confess our sins and
faults and so discover the grace that we needed to minister to
the greater whole.

I especially looked forward to our team time before and after
our healing meetings. I knew that these gatherings would manifest God's genuine strength at work in our weakness. With one
another's help, we would have no need to struggle alone. I
wanted nothing more than for us to say together at the end of
our time: "We have honored God in these bodies (1 Corinthians 12:24); we have equipped the saints to build up Christ's
Body with integrity (Ephesians 4:12)."

Rick and Lucy, two more of my colleagues from North America, joined Bev, Jake and me. So did our hosts in the city, Carmen and Fernando. Each team member was a delight—each
brought blessed gifts and equally blessed weaknesses to our
healing team. As we prayed for the greater gatherings, we also
prayed for each other in the specific areas in which we most
needed it.

I loved Rick's earnest desire to break out of his self-concern
and into relationship with real women. He had lost his father
early on, became the "good boy" for his religious mother and alternated between same-sex attraction and overly eager connection with women that burned out fast. At twenty-six years old, he
was frustrated in his longing to be a good gift to others.

As he shared, it became apparent that his devotional maturity still outweighed his relational skills. He tended to assess
women based on how much each one enhanced him: be it physical beauty, cleverness or piety. He knew that the main goal of
two becoming one is to grow in love with another—to offer

oneself generously and consistently to another. Still, he struggled. He wanted to see a woman as one worthy of love, not one
who existed to successfully enhance his image. That was his
prayer—the small yet stirring desire of his heart.

Rick needed mentors en route to maturity—to discover the
way of love in heterosexual relations. Fearful of failure, he had
burrowed himself in a world of faith that had left him flabby,
unfit to offer himself to another. It also resulted in dismissing
really fine women. We prayed for a new vision of what heterosexual relationships could be, and he promised to keep working it out once our time together was done.

Lucy's conflict was different but related. She had burrowed
deeply into an intensive community founded on prayer and
ministry to the poor. As a high-functioning woman with limited romantic experience with men, she defended her singleness as a form of freedom. Like the apostle Paul, she would refuse entanglement with domestic concerns in order to serve
Jesus more. But actually, she was afraid. At the core of her fear
was what she perceived as injustice at the core of "you-me" relating. Some get chosen, some not. She cited tearfully an early
rejection from a boy she desired; she began to piece together
this and other reasons she had chosen to defend herself from
romantic involvement with men. I asked her once if God had
given her the unique grace of celibacy, Paul's extraordinary gift
from God that enabled him to live without exclusive sexual and
emotional partnership with another. She did not know.

I conveyed to her my experience with a good friend and how
his call to celibacy did not bar him from offering himself heartily to the opposite-sex; it necessitated it! She looked a little confused but agreed to ponder the question with her community.
She was asking the right questions and recovering some real
answers for her sexual future.

Maybe the highlight of the trip was reengaging with our hosts Carmen and Fernando, a married couple in their late-twenties who had wed a few years earlier. Both loved Jesus, were capable and reliable individuals, and had served the Body well with their many gifts. They had also lost touch with one another.

The birth of their child cemented the parallel lives they were living. Both had intense jobs and so when one was not working they were parenting while the other worked. Instead of being one flesh, they had become roommates who rarely engaged together at meaningful spiritual and emotional levels. Sex was the last thing on either of their minds.

I could see trouble ahead, and when given a chance, both admitted they saw it too. She resented him for withholding attention; he claimed no access. We spoke of creative ways of connecting in light of their new family member. But more than that, Carmen and Fernando were able to catch their breath and experience afresh the breath of God upon their love for each other. We as a team prayed for the couple. It is easy for God to renew spouses as gifts for the other. "We waited for years to find each other; then when we gained access we lost each other." Both seemed relieved to have rediscovered what God had given them and yet what they had been sadly missing.

During our conference, we encountered many different types of people and need. But what stood out most were the many younger ones who really wanted answers—how to love Jesus and others well in light of the power of their sexuality and their call to be good gifts to each other.

God moved powerfully through his Spirit in teachings, testimonies and ministry times. Some were released from the shame of bad choices. More than that, God gave each a vision of the truth that they were destined to be a good offering to others, an offering that could grow in wisdom and maturity, a gift that in its offering to others could bear fruit that remains.

During those five days, the team prayed for one another and ministered to others. Given my own loneliness and vulnerability, I needed them; this weary house needed the house of God! In truth, we needed one another and God provided for us.

GRATEFUL FOR MERCY

Mercy flowed through our mutual reliance upon one another. I prayed that God would leave that deposit behind us. Gratefully, several of the local churches had made a commitment to meeting weekly in small groups to continue to work out what God had quickened in the conference. I was encouraged to return home—to my beautiful wife, as well as to a land living in the shadow of the House in need of help for its own houses. "Bring us down to size, O God, starting at the top," I prayed. "Let your judgment have its way. But in wrath, remember mercy."

All I had to do was think of how faithful he had been to me throughout my trip, despite my weakness. He kept me clean, not through any merit of my own, but through mercy. I meditated upon Psalm 116 on the plane ride home and wept at these words: "The Lord is gracious and righteous; / our God is full of compassion. / The Lord protects the simplehearted; / when I was in great need, he saved me. / Be at rest once more, O my soul, / for the Lord has been good to you" (Psalm 116:5-7).

Mercy alone had set me free. Instead of destroying my house due to my sin, he marked it with his blood and made a way for me to live and to become fruitful in communion with him and others. He had made the difference for me, through his mercy.

I thought of the team flying home with me: Lucy discovering who she was in relation to men, Rick emerging out of same-sex attraction and into whole-enough friendship with women, Jake and his recovery from porn addiction, and Bev from sexual abuse and a recent series of lesbian relationships. I thought too of Fernando and Carmen, holding down the fort in South America while seeking to recover intimacy at this phase of their life together. I prayed for mercy for all six: mercy in God's house to them, and mercy through them to others. (Remember these six! I will be charting their recovery throughout this book.)

My tears intensified into a sob. Trying to hide my blubbering gratitude, I averted the gaze of a cool-looking, young flight attendant whose severe henna-red hair belied her customary blue uniform. She would have none of it: "What are you reading? Psalm 116?" she asked. I nodded and she promptly, without a moment's notice, yanked the back of her uniform's collar down, exposing a tattooed cross with "PS 116" emblazoned at its center.

"God rescued this house alright," she said, misty-eyed. "You're reading my favorite psalm." We said only a few words to each other during the rest of the flight. And yet we shared a deep knowing. Though years and cultures apart, we were a part of one Body. Our temples housed the same God who had reclaimed us and made us his own.

2

WHOSE HOUSE ARE YOU?

DECLARING HIS DOMAIN

The Lord himself will establish a house for you.

2 SAMUEL 7:11

He anointed us, set his seal of ownership on us, and put his Spirit in our hearts as a deposit, guaranteeing what is to come.

2 CORINTHIANS 1:21-22

Lucy liked ministry, though she struggled with the "tent-making" required to serve in ministry. (This is the same Lucy described in the last chapter who served on the team and was questioning her call to celibacy.) Often insecure, especially in worldly settings like her job in retail, she was inclined to think of herself as inferior and irrelevant to the hipsters around her.

The guys were especially hard for her. They "rated" the female customers in the store constantly on their sex appeal, using

clever vulgarities. The guys knew she was a Christian. Yet the
cross on her neck meant different things to different coworkers.
To some it was just a tradition without profound meaning. They
were clueless as to what the cross meant to Lucy.

Then one day, one of the guys made some sexually sugges-
tive comments to her. Something indignant arose in her, and
she knew she had to give an answer for the cross around her
neck—for who she was as a Christian—and the implications of
that for her sexuality.

Lucy had been studying Ephesians, and was astounded by
Paul's description of what Jesus had won for her. "Because of
his great love for us, God, who is rich in mercy, made us alive
with Christ even when we were dead in transgressions" (Ephesians 2:4-5). His dying for her never ceased to soften her heart.
She knew she could be hard and critical in her insecurity; Jesus'
blood invited her back to mercy.

Meditation upon his rising, and how she was now raised
with Christ and seated with him in the heavenly realms (Ephesians 2:6), empowered her. God began to answer Paul's prayer
for the Ephesians in 1:17-18 in Lucy's life. She began to understand the fullness of what Jesus had won for her, that she was
God's "glorious inheritance" (Ephesians 1:18). *What?* She
thought: *he went through all that agony to claim me as his inheritance?* That challenged how she tended to see herself—a "nobody" on the lower end of the world's ladder.

In fact, she was a gift to the Creator and Redeemer of the uni-
verse. And in truth, a gift from him to others. Lucy had some
work to do in weeding out the worldliness of her thinking. Under
the old system, she agreed with how others marginalized her.
The cross declared something else—that she was a prize, a trea-
sure worth pursuing. The cross said it all. God went the distance
to reclaim her because he wanted her. And as one who believed

it, she was becoming alive to "that incomparably great power" (Ephesians 1:19) that propelled Jesus out of the tomb.

Acting on that strength, Lucy looked right at her coworker and said gently but firmly: "Please don't treat me as an assortment of body parts. I am a Christian. That means that I am defined by Christ. He has raised me up with him, given me the same Father he has. So please don't reduce me to something else. I don't like it and neither does my Father."

He got the message. The cross around her neck took on new meaning for both of them. The cross defined the nature of Lucy's "house." In the same way that the cross atop a steeple makes it clear that the building is a house of God, so can the cross define one's body as the house where God dwells with his Spirit. It communicates in an instant: my life is bound up in Another's. This house belongs to God.

I never cease to be amazed at the everyday power of the cross. A young gay man came up to me in Manhattan the other day and remarked on the beauty of the cross around my neck. All I could say was that it defines me. "He died; I died. He lives and so do I. What I seek to be and do now is under another power—the power of Jesus and his love."

FREEDOM FROM ACCUSATION

The cross conveys the power of Jesus' blood to make our house his own. That liberates a power to love others well, and clearly. Love flows from his crucified body to us and through us to others. That begins with knowing who we are. And who we are is founded on whose we are. We are his children, sons and daughters of the heavenly Father. Paul writes: "Now he [the Father] has reconciled you by Christ's physical body through death to present you holy in his sight, without blemish and free from accusation" (Colossians 1:22).

It's hard to engage openly and kindly with others when under the power of accusing voices. One constantly awaits judgment from others. We even begin to read in judgment when it's not there; our social interactions begin and often end with the skewed perception that we are neither welcomed nor wanted.

You met Bev in the last chapter as well. Bev had lived under that veil of accusation. An ungodly shame marked her life. In spite of a conservative Christian upbringing, she lived under the threat of nearly constant exposure and rejection. Part of this shame involved the sexual abuse she had experienced from her uncle. He was adept at seeing her, waiting for the right time, then violating her. After each horrific episode, he would push her away, not unlike Amnon who hated his sister Tamar more than he loved her after raping her (2 Samuel 13:15). As a helpless, damaged child, Bev became for her uncle a symbol of his shame and perversion. She reminded him of his own unrestrained evil; he hated her for it, thus adding insult to injury.

One cannot begin to fully grasp the power of that kind of injury and its impact upon one's way of seeing and interpreting others. Bev bore the perversion and the rejection of another; its depth reached into the very foundation of her humanity. But this form of abuse was not the only factor in her shame. Cultural and familial patterns contributed significantly to other false judgments. Bev observed that her brothers were highly favored in the household and given more opportunities to excel than she was. Women in her family received favor for physical beauty and appeal, as well as for humble, holy service. She felt caught between the sexiness required of her and yet also that call to holiness!

But sexy meant abuse and ultimately more rejection. When Bev brought up to her mother how she did not want to be around her uncle anymore, her mother accused Bev of disrespect. After that, she refused to speak about what was happening.

EYES OF SHAME

Complicating matters further was the Christian community around her. Bev's family, including her uncle, was foundational to the life of the local fellowship. It is no small miracle of grace that she grew up loving Jesus; in truth, she could not imagine life without him. At the same time she learned early on that in church, family honor mattered more than justice. It was better to keep secrets that might shame the family name than to tell the truth. Period.

Far from her family at university, she needed kindness. Bev offered little resistance to the sensual comfort afforded by her "friend" there. The power of that bond floored her. Never before had she felt loved so deeply. Never before had she felt such shame. The intensity of her needs for acceptance and understanding only heightened her guilt. Her friend's eyes of love became eyes that also exposed her shame. It was hopeless; she felt helpless, not unlike the child subject to abuse. Only now she was the consenting partner. She was adding insult to injury by violating her own moral code.

Bev articulated: "I discovered anger as the flipside of my helplessness. Anger helped me to do something, not just hate myself. Rage raised me up a bit from my depression. I loved the Psalms, the way David would feel awful about life then shout out his lament to God. I too was being 'forced to restore what I did not steal!' (Psalm 69:4) I did a lot of shouting in those days."

She hated her uncle for robbing her innocence. And she hated herself for participating in her own robbery: how she had perverted an otherwise life-giving friendship. She felt shame, real shame for the lines she had crossed with that woman. Now her body was ignited by powerful desire and a storehouse of images and memories. What she regretted, she also wanted. Badly.

But she wanted Jesus more. She missed him. In spite of all the craziness of her childhood, Jesus had revealed himself throughout those years as her refuge and strength, a high tower amid chaos. She wanted to secure that refuge again. Yet she could not go home for that. She had to find him afresh, in the reality of her new life.

HOMECOMING

Bev met a new friend in her apartment complex. Sue was a Christian, kind yet with no sexual or inordinate emotional need for Bev. At one point Bev became ill with a mild form of hepatitis and was out of commission for several months. Sue and some friends from their church served Bev in her apartment until she was better. It made the difference. Bev recovered physically through the love of the Body. Soon after, Bev began attending the church and discovered that a group was starting to meet to deal with sexual and relational issues. Sue helped Bev out along the way. That made a difference; Bev trusted Sue, but not the whole church.

Healing started slowly. Sue and the group offered Bev a way forward to begin to rediscover Jesus: his mighty love for her and, in particular, a Christian way forward to sort out her sexuality and relationships. It took Bev a while to trust the church in that way. In the same way that distrust of the church came through those who preferred the honor of men over Jesus' honor, she began, slowly but surely, to trust new friends in the church who served people by meeting them at their least honorable.

Bev began to see the church in a new light: God's house was becoming a place where she could begin to open the doors of her own house and receive good things. The cross began to take on new meaning for Bev in this process. In Colossians 2:14-15, Paul describes how on the cross, Jesus' broken body "canceled the written code, with its regulations, that was against us and that stood opposed to us. . . . Having disarmed the powers and authorities, he made a public spectacle of them, triumphing over them by the cross."

Through the Son's body, the Father made a way for us to be free. That freedom applies to two kingdoms: the kingdom of religion—the power of the law to condemn us, and the kingdom of paganism—how our devotion to falsehood deceives and defiles us. Jesus was crucified by the highest expression of religious law—the Pharisees, and by the highest expression of paganism—the Roman Empire. He surrendered to their murder of him. But he turned the tables. His broken body and shed blood cancelled out both the power of the religious law to condemn us, and the power of the most exquisite paganisms to tempt us to worship at their altars. The cross crushed the authority of both legalism and license to define the saints. He triumphed over both on the cross.

MOVING TO THE TRUE REFUGE

As I consider myself and most of my colleagues, I would say we have been harassed and accused by both legalism and license. On the one hand, many of us were raised in conservative households. Most know the truth about Jesus and believe it. And some, like Bev, were subject to heavy-handed religion in which the appearance of order counted more than what was actually going on in the "holy" house.

At the same time, all of us were subject to the material and sensual excesses of our modern culture—idols that beckoned to us constantly and took many religious ones captive. We did not forsake the one true religion; we just made other altars and tried to hide them from our communities of faith.

We hide in Jesus' name, and the church becomes a false refuge for us. How? We tell no one of the dishonorable things that we do or that have happened to us. Why? We value the appearance of honor over godly honor! We would rather look good than be good. So we uphold the letter of the law, at times with an intensity that persuades us temporarily that we are holy.

We lose the cross in this equation. Fiery preaching is helpful only when it leads us to the cross. There alone do we discover the "great exchange"—Jesus' blood for our "sin-sickness," grace for dishonor. The cross alone stills the shameful and accusatory voice.

Bev needed to discover the cross in her new community of faith. She knew what the cross meant abstractly, but had never actually worked out its meaning with others. That is a huge shift for anyone who grew up in an honor-based culture. In the latter, the most dishonorable thing you can do is tell a messy truth that may threaten to dishonor others. Yet in that community she discovered a liberating truth: godly honor only comes through Jesus and the way he exchanges what is truly dishonorable for his grace.

What was happening to Bev was clear: her house was becoming marked by the cross. And in that definition, she was beginning to rest. She felt protected. She felt comfort in her relationships without the threat of violation. She felt as if God, through his house, was offering her both his justice and his mercy. She could begin to exhale. The cross discovered in his house made a profound difference for her "house."

Few communities offer this to the sexually and relationally broken. But churches who do offer this kind of hope fulfill Paul's command to the church in 1 Corinthians 12. There he implored stronger members of the one body to take special care of weaker ones. "Those parts of the body that seem to be weaker are indispensable, and the parts that we think are less honorable we treat with special honor. And the parts that are unpresentable are treated with special modesty. . . . God has combined the members of the body and has given greater honor to the parts that lacked it" (1 Corinthians 12:22-24).

Bev was learning to entrust her dishonorable parts with trustworthy members of the Body. She found those capable of meeting her with dignity and going with her to the cross. There they discovered the One who exchanges shame for beauty, accusation for confirmation. Jesus turns the tables on honor-based cultures; he in his body gives greater honor to the parts that lack it.

On occasion, when we pray together as a team, we anoint each other with oil. We may make the sign of the cross on the forehead of each member. I noticed that every time we prayed for Bev in that way, she wept. I asked her what that meant to her. "It reminds me of what he did for me . . . how what my uncle did and what I did are no match for what God did—how he acted on my behalf. And how you guys who know all that stuff are there believing for me and helping me to believe it through loving me, and reminding me of that love by doing stuff like signing me with the cross. It helps . . ." she trailed off, still weeping.

Named by God as a daughter of favor, signed and sealed by his cross, Bev is growing in her authority to refuse accusation, and exchange dishonor for his acceptance.

A MORE POWERFUL INTIMACY

The cross plows a deep furrow through both license and legalism. Jesus' bloody death has power to lay claim to us once more as children of divine favor. In so doing, the crucified God is also the powerful Jesus, overturning the "altars" of religious performance and illicit pleasure in our own houses of worship. The cross shows us love—the distance God endured to reclaim us as his own. And it manifests power to reclaim us as the very temple in which he wills to dwell. In short, the cross grants us power to become sons and daughters of favor. Jake needed this power badly.

Jake had been the son of favor. Doted on by his mother, indulged by his father, Jake grew up without good boundaries and a focused, disciplined will. His religion was Christian but actually he worshiped at the altars of pagan gods and goddesses. Internet pornography intrigued him from early on, as did playing around with girls without "going too far." (That means not having actual intercourse while indulging in everything else under the sun. Who knew legalism could be so "gymnastic"?)

He was handsome, gifted, and possessed a charming, casual demeanor that put others at ease. He was a natural for church leadership roles. His father, a quiet man with a quiet history of adultery, was proud of his son's early success in ministry and in scoring women. Like many men of his generation, he had a strong tolerance "for guys to be guys," and so winked at the apparent inconsistencies of his holy and profane son.

You could say that Jake was a superficial Christian. He had inherited his faith from a wounded set of parents. In truth, he had yet to actually make the faith his own. So it did not take long for his natural charisma to get him into trouble. In truth, he was using the power of his position as a young adult leader to meet and use women, both emotionally and physically.

Thankfully, he had a wise and engaging pastor who saw the trouble and intervened. Jake had a crisis of faith—his first. All came out. The pastor checked out his Web data and found hundreds of porn sites Jake had frequented. Several young women attested to being confused by his odd blend of encouragement and sensuality; most had left the church when he went on to the next female "disciple." Jake had a choice: get serious with God or move on. By God's grace, Jake woke up to the power of sin, and he responded to Jesus' call to follow him, to discover for the first time what it meant to be signed by the cross as the defining, saving reality of his life.

Like he did for Nehemiah, God freed Jake to see the damage done and cry out: "You see the trouble we are in; I lie in ruins, and my gates have been burned with fire. Come let us rebuild the walls so that we will no longer be in disgrace" (Nehemiah 2:17).

Jake rightfully saw that his disgrace was at once personal and corporate; others had been disgraced by his sin, and needed healing from his influence. He submitted to a rigorous process of restoration, which you could say was his first serious endeavor as a follower of Jesus. This was the first battle he had actually waged in Christ. The lines were simple. He wanted Jesus, and chose to combat the old sloppy freedoms of sensual license.

Jake faced a real challenge. Would he welcome the grace that has power to make all things new—would he be reconciled "by Christ's physical body through death" to be presented "holy . . . without blemish, free from accusation" (Colossians 1:22)? And at the same time, would Jake fulfill the condition Paul gave to those who would walk free from sin and accusation? Would he, like the apostle, "continue in [the] faith, established and firm, unmoved from the hope held out in the gospel" (Colossians 1:23)?

THE CHALLENGE OF THE CROSS

For Lucy, Bev and Jake, the challenge of holding fast to the cross involved discovering the relevance of the crucified One to their sexual identities. That gospel "hope" Paul described in Colossians has profound relevance to who we are as "body" people. We possess bodies, physical frames that house longings for love and physical connection with others. The sexual dimension of our humanity is central to our "body lives."

Yet our sexuality also creates conflict for us. That conflict may be relatively mild, as it was for Lucy in her fear of rejection from men. Sexuality may involve a strange blend of fear and uncharted, confusing pleasures, as it had for Bev. Or it may involve how one masters obvious and powerful habit patterns, as in Jake's case. Regardless, the conflict may tempt us to split off from our bodies altogether. We may try to resolve the conflict by separating flesh from spirit.

Jesus does not give us that option. Paul made it really clear to the Corinthians—"you are the body of Christ" (1 Corinthians 12:27). In other words, you are inseparably joined with Jesus Christ. In the Body. In fact, you are the Body, his Body on earth. The Body matters.

LOSING THE GOSPEL

Paul could not have been more insistent on this point. In their detachment from the body, the church at Corinth risked losing the whole gospel. Let me explain. I alluded to this earlier in the first chapter but it bears detailing. The Corinthians opposed the unity of body and spirit for reasons not unlike those held by our three friends. The most obvious reason involved sexual immorality. Some of the Corinthians were still frequenting prostitutes and justified such immorality on the grounds that it was basic and natural to the needs of the body. "Everything is permissible . . . food for the stomach and the stomach for food" (1 Corinthians 6:12-13). To them such culturally accepted behavior posed little conflict with the affairs of the Spirit.

In truth, we could assume it actually posed a significant conflict for them. They just employed a common defense to resolve the conflict: a form of dualism in which the flesh (bodily sexuality) is separated from the high and lofty things of the Spirit. Their response to Paul's concerns over their "fleshly" habits: "What we do with our bodies operates separately from the spiritual and poses no threat to our newfound faith."

Another extreme group arose. They wanted nothing to do with bodily affairs at all; they dealt with their bodily conflicts by denying them. They acted as if they had transcended the body altogether. To them the body was an unnecessary appendage to be forsaken for life in the Spirit.

Paul addresses both sets of errors. They derived from the same source—a gnostic dualism that tried to separate spirituality from sexuality. He challenges this dualism in 1 Corinthians 6:12-20 and 1 Corinthians 15. His thesis: the body is meant for the Lord (1 Corinthians 6:13), and our bodies are members of Christ himself (1 Corinthians 6:15). Paul's answer is foundational to all Christians. He is in essence saying: "You have become the living, breathing, feeling body of Christ—you are united with him in all that you are—what you do, think and feel."

That involves the sexual component of the body. That means that our choices concerning the body have huge implications. We either glorify him in the body or desecrate him. Paul lays out the whole of the gospel message in his call to us to take seriously what it means to be the body of Christ. Jesus has bought each body with his blood; he laid claim to us as his own and became rightful owner of the temple. His crucifixion has authority to challenge our "right" to do whatever we want in the body (1 Corinthians 6:19-20). Furthermore, Jesus in his resurrection has filled our bodies with his very Spirit, thus raising us up for what he desires for us (1 Corinthians 6:14, 19).

And his desire for the body matters because we have become his Body—both as individual believers, and as the one Body of Christ, the church.

Paul also speaks of God's future plan for the body. Here he takes stern issue with the Corinthian belief that the body had no lasting value. Paul challenges the popular idea that the body and its sexuality are just like "food for the stomach"; he makes the case that God will destroy them both but will raise up the body for eternal purposes (1 Corinthians 6:14).

The apostle asserts God's plan for the body, not only now but also in the life to come. For the Corinthians to dismiss the body as immaterial to God's full plan and purpose was the same as denying Christ's resurrection from the dead (1 Corinthians 15:16, 19). To Paul, the body of the believer would undergo the same rhythm as Jesus' body: crucified with him and raised with him in this life. Yet not entirely. The Corinthian believer had to prepare in the body now for the final resurrection that would occur with the death and transformation of the human body into its new and final form.

That meant two key realities. First, the Corinthians were not free to act as if they were "heavenly bodies"—fully united with Christ and thus free from the demands of the body on earth. Those who postured as wholly realized spiritual beings deceived themselves. Jesus had laid claim to them in the present, but the consummation of full intimacy with Christ belonged in the age to come.

For the likes of Bev and Lucy, that meant having to make peace with their reality as "body people." Lucy wanted to forego her need for love from others, especially men. For Bev, the body and its desires simply meant trouble—the threat of assault, the distortion of desire in same-sex attraction. For both women, the body meant shame and exposure. But they knew enough about his love to trust what he desired for them.

Jesus' call to know him in the body and to learn to honor him in the body ("Therefore honor God with your body," 1 Corinthians 6:20) presents a challenge. It means being reconciled to our needs for intimacy—needs for both God and our fellow humanity.

LIVE FOR TOMORROW

The second challenge from 1 Corinthians 6 involves sexual immorality and eternity. Here Paul stresses the importance of eternity in lending urgency to how we steward the body today. Our future—resurrected, embodied humanity—ought to inform our present behavior. Take the long view of the body—life with God forever. To the Corinthians who were unsure of the resurrection of the human body from the dead, Paul wanted to be really clear. An eternal tomorrow matters today in regards to the body.

He elaborates on this in great detail in 1 Corinthians 15. Citing the import of Jesus' resurrection and their own impending resurrection from the dead, the apostle implored them to stop sinning against the body: "If the dead are not raised, 'Let us eat and drink, for tomorrow we die'" (1 Corinthians 15:32). Paraphrasing, Paul warns all who listen: "You are acting ignorantly of the body and its eternal destiny. Stop sinning against Jesus and the body and prepare for the life yet to come!"

For Jake, drowsy and addicted to the pleasures of the flesh, he needed to wake up to the power of the body. Like the Corinthians, he had justified his immorality on the basis of a bad habit common to humanity. Aware of his self-deception, Jake still doubted whether or not he could get free from such a deep network of desire and habit. Yet he was growing to trust this Jesus with the whole of his life, including his sexuality. God used the clear teaching of scripture to awaken Jake's conscience. Thankfully, culture and habit do not determine true sexual ethics; Jesus does. But what he asks of us, he enables us to realize. His blood makes us his own, and his Spirit fills us with power from on high, confirming whose we are and what we are for.

RECLAIM THE GOSPEL

"The body is not meant for sexual immorality, but for the Lord, and the Lord for the body" (1 Corinthians 6:13). For Paul, the body has power to manifest Jesus. In all of its properties, including the sexual, the body could make known his grace or deflect that grace, in truth, make a mockery of it. ("Shall I then take the members of Christ and unite them with a prostitute? Never!" 1 Corinthians 6:15.) The sexual "beliefs" of the Corinthians had power to distort the central tenets of the gospel itself. Their split between body and spirit threatened their grasp of the cross and its power: Christ crucified to make us wholly his own, Christ resurrected to reconcile us to all that is good and true about our humanity.

Their faulty sexual beliefs also revealed the failure to grasp what it means to be the church. We are joined with him, body, soul and spirit. We actually represent him as his body on earth, "his glorious inheritance in the saints" (Ephesians 1:18). In splitting their bodies from their spiritual lives, the Corinthians became vulnerable to withholding from, or dehumanizing, one another, as well as defiling the very One who had made them his own.

I do not exaggerate then by concluding that in matters of sexual integrity and purity, the whole gospel is at stake. We cannot dismiss what we do with the body and still claim to be truthful Christians. The Body of Christ, manifest in both individual believers and corporate gatherings, is intended to be the dwelling place for the wonder-working power of the cross. If that power is not manifest in our sexual lives, then we have not grasped Jesus' saving work at the level for which he intended it. But conversely, for those of us who have come to trust and know him in our sexuality, Jesus manifests the power of the cross to make us his own. We in turn become glorious expressions of his house, his living, breathing Body on earth.

"The body is meant for the Lord, and the Lord of the body." That verse took on new and powerful meaning for me one eventful weekend. And it remains the clarion call of Christ upon the whole of my identity in this body.

RECLAIM THE BODY

Maybe a brief story will help illustrate how central this truth is to me. Had I not surrendered my house and all of its longings to the Lord, I would not be a Christian today. As a new Christian, I vacillated constantly between my new life in the body and my old life as a practicing homosexual. One night, weary after a frustrating gathering with believers ("does anyone understand my life?"), I determined to go out and land a one-night stand. I rediscovered the truth—it's easy to have sex, hard to secure love. After the rush (and departure of whomever), I lay in my bed in the early morning hours and wept. My body felt like a temple of death. I felt the death of sin in my body. I did not try to sweeten the moment with drugs or alcohol. I just felt sin's consequence. That I knew Jesus and forsook him grieved me more than the violation of a principle. I had violated him in this body.

Certain that I was hopeless, that Christianity for me was a vain attempt at a better life, I resolved to sleep off the despair and wake up to an unbelieving life. Fat chance. I could not sleep and the only thing that came to mind was a sweet and somewhat inane worship song. For some reason, I began to sing out that three-chord wonder, right there on my bed. As I did, the Holy Spirit filled the room. It was the presence of the Father and his Son, joining me in my distress. Their presence, however awesome, revealed my filth. I felt dirty; I was dirty. God provided in a way I could grasp. Through the eyes of my heart, I perceived rain falling from the ceiling, a light gentle rain that nevertheless had power to wash me. It rained for a few minutes as the Lord cleansed me.

I could not understand God. I thought: *Why so loving? Why do you give me something good in exchange for dirt?* I tried singing out my gratitude but could not. Tears of gratitude were my only offering and finally I slept.

I awoke a few hours later to someone banging on the door; it was my one Christian friend in the area, urging me to come with him to church. I told him all that had happened. He said simply: "The Lord is making you his own through his mercy. He has made you his own, and he will keep on making you his own until you get it—you belong to him." With that, he took off the cross he was wearing and put it on me. "Just a reminder of whose you are." I wear it to this day.

Thirty years later, I identify still as one who belongs to God through the authority of the cross. Jesus has freed me, in season and out, single and married, in times of freedom from sexual conflict and in seasons full of it, to submit myself to the One who seeks only my good. Truly, the cross has freed me to not forsake my sexuality but rather to offer it to him. Since that divine encounter on my bed, I have not shied away from conversing with God freely about my longings for love and connection contained within this body.

The psalmist understands this passion and its relevance to the spiritual life. "On my bed I remember you; I think of you through the watches of the night. Because you are my help, I sing in the shadow of your wings. My soul clings to you; your right hand upholds me" (Psalm 63:6-8). Often in bed, in the place we often associate with intimacy, I offer to the Lord my sexual longings. Although unguarded, and in a way exposed, I abide with him there and declare: "I am yours, O God, and I entrust these desires to you, however frustrated or skewed or exaggerated." I can agree with the psalmist when he declares: "All my longings lie open before you" (Psalm 38:9).

I know he hears my honest prayers and will act. He will elevate my desires where they are too low, burn off childish ones, and refine those pleasing to him. I am confident that he will open his hand, and satisfy these desires in his time and in his way, as he delights in fulfilling the desires of those who fear him (Psalm 145:16, 19).

It is a work in progress, to be sure. And yet through the cross, my house rests secure. His finished work at Calvary defines my temple; it reminds me constantly of the love that frees me to be loved, and to love others purely. The cross has made my house honorable. And it gives me the assurance that what is yet dishonorable will be changed. He will complete the good work he has begun in me.

3

LAYING A SURE FOUNDATION

LOVE'S DESCENT

Unless the LORD builds the house,

its builders labor in vain.

PSALM 127:1

But one should be careful how he builds. For no one can lay any foundation other than the one already laid, which is Christ Jesus.

1 CORINTHIANS 3:10-11

In order to offer ourselves responsibly to others, we need a sure foundation. A strong base means a stable house. Foundations help determine how many rooms may be built upon it and thus how many lives the house might contain. A sure foundation for the building of the human "house" is based on love. We love others well when we have been loved well. Secure in love and empowered by it, we are fit to know how and when to open our "house" up to others. Our foundations exert huge influence upon our sexual and relational lives.

The cross conveys the power of that foundational love: One has offered himself to us wholly, without reserve. He poured out his life to lay a new foundation for our lives. Truly his life of forgiving, delivering, and healing, resulting in a bloody death, provides the base for a new life of love for us. The cross equally conveys the power of his resurrection: he catapulted out of the tomb in order to demonstrate his power to raise upon that foundation a new humanity.

That's what the cross means for our "houses"—Jesus Christ lays a new foundation of love on which the broken bases of men and women can become solid, able to sustain loving relationships. The cross points to the goal—loving like Jesus—and the means toward that end—Jesus himself. As he becomes the primary relationship in our lives, he helps us to identify the gaps in our foundations and to shore them up with perfect love. That provides a new base on which to learn how to love others well. The cross around our necks is the steeple upon the "house church"—it means that we have opened the doors to Love himself. He has entered our frame and is intent on laying a foundation of love in our depths. The cross means that Love himself seeks to manifest himself through the whole of that self, from the ground floor up.

Maybe that's why I cringe when celebrities who sport huge crosses pervert that love. I remember one rapper on an award show who sang while simulating sex acts on stage. He gave Jesus all the glory when he won the award. Wow. It is easy to wear the symbol, and easier still to distort its meaning in how we live.

Thank God that he bears with us; he gives us the grace of time in which to engage with the meaning of the cross—its actual relevance to the choices we make in our pursuit of love.

It takes time for the ornament to order us. We are naturally disordered in love, subject to bypassing the "real meal" for some junk food.

REAL GAPS

Each of us has gaps in the foundations of our "houses." Those gaps are hungry; like a vacuum, they detect and absorb sources of love. Or at least the appearance of love. Our gaps do not discriminate well, especially at the beginning of our "cross-walk." Our faulty foundations incline us toward evil. Yet take heart: shiny objects that beckon to us and appeal to gaps in our foundations are no match for the power of the cross. He is intent on descending into our depths in order to establish us in love!

I discovered this at a profound level when I began to minister to others coming out of homosexuality many years ago. One young man sought my help, and over the course of his meeting with me began to act seductively. At first I thought he was only being friendly and engaging. Guess again. Shamefully, I admit that I liked the attention and wanted to linger a while in the unspoken provocation at hand. This man was handsome, and appeared to be both tender and strong. He appealed to some profound need in me. His advances coincided with gaps in my foundation.

Then Jesus took ahold of me; my eye caught the large cross hanging on the wall across the room. Jesus beckoned to me upon the cross. Risen, his wounds yet visible, his presence empowered me to live the truth. I straightened up in my resolve to finish the introductory meeting by making it clear to the young man that our groups were designed for the purpose of coming out of homosexuality.

That night, I struggled with a profound ache for masculine love. My imagination alternated between that man and Jesus.

My body wanted sexual release but I knew that masturbation would not satisfy my need. Deeper still was a longing for love. I slept holding a cross to my chest. Jesus covered me. I slept fitfully and dreamed that I was hanging onto the cross amid a fierce wind. I awoke in peace, the sexual temptation having subsided.

At the time, I lived with my parents. I was reminded the next morning of the still awkward relationship with my father. Though I love him very much, the connection then was strained. That combined with a history of belittlement in other male relationships composed a foundational gap in me. It fueled my same-sex attraction. My counselor and I had been exploring some of these relationships; I was learning to identify the historic ways I interpreted them, how I would often shut down and draw faulty conclusions about these male figures. I needed love from men; yet I also realized that in my brokenness and self-protection I resisted it. That resistance perverted my need. I found it easier to sexualize my need rather than to pursue it rightfully. Better to fantasize than to risk rejection.

I needed love. That morning I prayed. During the prayer time, Jesus brought up a series of pictures of men who had a hand in my salvation: not only in the initial decision to follow Jesus but who had encouraged me at different phases of my salvation. I was amazed. Faithful men loved me well; faithful men, tender and strong, stood with me in all my weakness and brokenness and called out the good in me. They saw more than I did and blessed it.

I wept. Still holding the cross, I asked the Lord to remove the defensive barrier that barred me from fully receiving this good love. As I continued to pray, I saw a picture of my walking with Jesus on a pathway. We were soon joined with another man, a Christian friend. I felt uncertain about this friendship, as if I might need him too much or be rejected. Jesus' presence was strong and assuring: "Keep walking!" The ground we trod was solid. I could see that on either side of us were men flailing about in what appeared to be quicksand. They were trapped by their relationships, and going under. I felt deeply grieved, but was also aware that Jesus was preparing me to help them.

"Walk with me as you seek to love your brothers and I will keep the ground you walk on solid and sure. As you walk with them—giving and receiving—you too will become solid and sure." That seemed to be his message to me. And it has proven to be true. Over the last thirty years, I have pressed into cross-centered friendships that have been pure, deeply satisfying, and fruitful for his service.

Jesus, working through his Body, enabled me to perceive and receive the love I needed in order to become a solid man. He has been faithful to emblazon the cross around my neck upon the foundation of my soul. He has made my house secure in love—secure enough, anyway. He has freed me to welcome the love that is truly there and to love others out of that solid place.

To be set free for real love, we must face our need for love, especially in historic areas of neglect or hurt. These foundational gaps require our attention. They certainly provoke the attention of the crucified One who died to demonstrate to us the "love that surpasses knowledge" and who rose from the dead so that we might "be filled to the measure of all [his] fullness" (Ephesians 3:19). That fullness is nothing less than unfailing love.

We need that love. Toni Dolfo-Smith, beloved colleague and healing pioneer, writes beautifully about how whole-enough parents function as God's arm in meeting the needs of their children—needs for attention and affirmation and affection which, when satisfied, result in a confident and much loved human being. Bearing that solid foundation, one can persevere unto maturity, and love others well.

In order for these needs to be met, children require a two-party system—a mother and a father. A child needs both masculine and feminine love. That is especially clear in his or her acquisition of a healthy gender identity. A child needs to be awakened to the good of their own gender by the same-sex parent, and granted a clear, trustworthy vision of the opposite gender through the opposite-sex parent. Through two cooperative parents who hold each other accountable to raise the one they created, children become secure and empowered in love. They navigate well the journey to sexual and relational wholeness.

In the fallen world of family we each grew up in, that scenario never happens perfectly. Neglect and abuse are two possibilities in that damaged scenario.

Neglect is the passive misuse of power. These are sins of omission. Through neglect, some of these needs simply are not met. Parents just don't have enough energy or well-being or time to adequately attend to their children. The resulting lack of affirmation and physical touch can lead to gaps in the child's foundation. Lacking confidence in oneself, the child may be more subject to poor choices about how to secure love and power, and be less likely to endure the hardships and self-denial required of the journey toward mature love.

Neglect on the one hand; abuse on the other. By abuse I mean active misuses of power. Here the parent commits the sin of commission. Through demeaning words, hard fists, or distorted relational patterns, the parent (or other authority figures) injects frightening, alien realities into the child's life. Toni writes, "At some point in our lives, others have broken and invaded our lives through force, manipulation, and humiliation. Such abuse plants unwanted feelings and experiences in our lives, which shapes how we see God and others. We may begin to view life as fearful, insecure, and uncertain."

As bearers of neglect (unmet needs for love) and abuse (insertion of damaging experiences), every human being possesses gaps in his or her foundation. Complicating matters is a stronghold of ungodly shame about these gaps. That shame may be twofold: disquiet about personal brokenness, as well as the shame we feel about discussing the failures of others, for example, the loved ones who neglected and abused us.

I experienced minimal shame about dealing with foundational brokenness. For that I credit my parents who were relatively healthy and willing to engage honestly about hard interpersonal issues. Another factor was cultural: the highly individualized and therapeutic culture of California, lends itself to such exploration. But most cultures in the United States and elsewhere oppose such an effort. Especially "honor-based" cultures in which one is defined primarily by their family of origin. That would apply to many non–Anglo Saxon cultures where people are much more defined by the group—the family—rather than by their experiences as individuals. There, one goes to great lengths to defend the honor of one's family, because one's own honor is bound up in the family's honor.

To tell the truth about the failure of a loved one dishonors oneself and the entire family in an honor-based culture. That was especially true for Carmen and Fernando, our hosts in the South American conference described in the first chapter. Both were from proud and apparently "upright" families. Both grew up with the unspoken rule of "family first": the family name and dignity was highly valued, and each member had a responsibility to uphold that dignity.

For Carmen, that meant coping silently with the reality of her parents' failed marriage. She was the eldest child of three who took care of her young siblings. She also cared for her mother who endured a decade of her husband's adultery, then a divorce. A traditional woman whose life was founded on her husband's, Carmen's mother had yet to recover from her marital wounds. She remained a desolate woman.

Carmen recalled her mother as depressed and understandably needy. She loved her mother a great deal and was hesitant to blame her for anything. But blame is different from looking at the effect of neglect and abuse in one's family. Carmen was neglected: her father withdrew from the family, which introduced fear and insecurity into her life. In response to his absence, she bonded with her mother in a kind of despair and resignation over the pain of living. She inherited her mother's tendency toward depression.

Carmen's emotional fragility was not apparent. Carmen remained a highly capable woman; she continued to be the disciplined caregiver who had learned early on to help close the gaps left by both mother and father. Although she gave love as best she could, she failed to receive the love she needed—need for attention, affection and affirmation. Neither parent adequately imparted that love to her. She carried those unmet needs and wounds into her adult life.

Carmen coped with her unmet needs with dignity. She lived a contained life, yet she became increasingly anxious, fearful and depressed after the birth of her first child. To husband Fernando, she seemed unreachable.

Fernando had his own gaps. His family had been similarly divided but for different reasons. His mother had been an alcoholic who died after a long battle with cirrhosis when he was ten years old. He recalled her dearly; she gave what she could, and his memories of her were precious to him. She did try, he asserted, and he carried those efforts in his heart. His father was distant and grew more so after his wife's death. Absent much of the time, he could be alternately indulgent and demanding when present. On the one hand, he commanded the boy to excel in school and sports, demands that could crack like a whip; on the other hand, he spoiled Fernando with lax oversight and material things. Fernando resented him as much as he wanted more of him.

A demanding job in business took his father out of the home for days at a time. A housekeeper cared for Fernando and his younger sister until Fernando left home for college. A saving grace for him came through the dynamic faith of this housekeeper. She was a devout Christian who prayed for the children faithfully and invited them to attend a parish in their town. Fernando's faith sustained him during these lean years at home. He was unattended and lonely; at times he struggled against Internet porn and misuse of alcohol. Yet he engaged with God as best as he could. (The parish offered little in the way of peer fellowship.) Fernando bore the neglect of his youth with dignity, as did Carmen. The two met in school, where they began a life together.

Like Carmen, Fernando's first instinct was to guard the family honor more than to expose its gaps. But he was now hurting. His job as an engineer frustrated him; he wanted more for his life but did not know how to attain it. Since the baby, life with Carmen was getting harder. She seemed sad and remote. He was dabbling again with Internet porn, and isolating from her. To Carmen, her husband seemed to be disappearing. His emotional absence triggered her fears of abandonment.

It was a privilege to meet these two on the ground of their gaps. It was inspired timing! As is often the case, God used normal life changes, in this case, a new baby, to reveal hindrances to a rich exchange of love in the present. God reveals these gaps in order to heal. He goes to great lengths to establish us in love.

The cross conveys precisely that great length; God went the distance for us at Calvary so that we might recover union with him and each other. "The cross gave me somewhere to go with the conflict I felt toward my family. I wanted to love them but couldn't, not from the heart. Yet the cross also put me in conflict. Jesus invited me to face what was really going—the distance I felt from my loved ones, even though we appeared so close," reflected Carmen.

Both Carmen and Fernando were learning the connection between admitting some foundational gaps in their "houses," and Jesus' capacity to meet them there. These two were better at feeling guilt for not having done their duty than they were at receiving mercy for their brokenness. Though good soldiers of the cross, they struggled to yield their wounds to his. Yet they knew this was their healing season, beginning with our conference. I urged them to just receive for themselves. They had new motivation: they did not want their gaps passed down to their child.

Having talked about the reality of wounds and needs, Carmen and Fernando considered what both the Father and Son endured at Calvary. This helped them to grasp further the meaning of the cross as it applied to specific gaps in their foundations. They began to "hear" God speaking to them through the cross: "I know your suffering; I know your neglect and abuse. I have endured the tearing between parent and child that you bear."

The cross is all about the tearing between Parent and Child. On the cross, the Father was wrenched from the Son, the Son from the Father. Jesus' agony is more familiar to us than the Father's. Having been deserted by his closest friends then abused unto death, Jesus held out for the consolation of his

Father. When sin veiled the face of his Father, Jesus despaired; his lament on the cross, "My God, why have you forsaken me?" (Matthew 27:46) represents our forsakenness as well.

In that lament, Jesus cries out on behalf of Carmen and Fernando and all who have faced wounds and needs rooted in broken family bonds. In that lament, he cries out on behalf of all who have endured the distance between mother and son, father and daughter, every gap between dependent child and parent. For those wounds, Jesus went the distance. He endured that gap—emotionally, physically, spiritually. He felt it. In his profound understanding and gentle presence, he frees us to feel its ache. He offers us himself, his forsakenness, his wound.

GOD OF THE GAPS

God knows the depth of the gaps. He is fully aware that the man and woman who created us were not able to meet all of our needs and ward off every misuse of power. Greed and selfishness, death, diseases of body and mind, addiction, war, infidelity, and divorce broke bonds with parents that might have satisfied our desires with good things. Jesus on the cross liberates our cries of forsakenness. He frees us to feel the ache for attention, for affirmation, for affection. Our cries have reached the heart of the Father. He has responded to those cries through the cries of his Son on the cross.

French philosopher Simone Weil wrote of the distance both the Father and the Son endured on the cross to close our gaps: "So that love might be as great as possible, the distance between Father and Son must be as great as possible. . . . This infinite distance between God and God, this supreme tearing apart, this agony above all others, this marvel of love, is the crucifixion."

The wound between Father and Son had to be great and

deep in order to assume the weight of our wound. Just as the
Father and Son suffered, so must we identify our own suffering. When our pain is veiled by denial or avoidance, we squan-
der the benefits of his wounds. We must hear afresh Jesus' cry
of forsakenness; it has power to quicken our own cry to the
Father. The Father hears that cry, as surely and as poignantly
as he heard the lament of his Son on the cross. The Father la-
mented his Son's agony. He suffered as much as the Son, maybe
more so, as his beloved descended into deep darkness—the
darkness of sin.

The Father's agony involved releasing his Son unto that darkness, without offering his consolation. *For the Father to withhold that consolation—that was the Father's supreme suffering.* In
order for divine love to realize its perfect work, the distance
between love and love had to be vast.

During one extended prayer time, Carmen, Fernando and I
waited at the cross together. We considered the wound sustained between the Father and the Son for our sake. We asked
for that marvel of love to have its perfect way in us. We asked
the Holy Spirit of the Father and Son to identify the particular
gaps he wanted to assume. We held fast to the psalmist's hope:
"Though my father and mother forsake me, the LORD will receive me" (Psalm 27:10).

The power of Jesus' blood to heal deep wounds took on new
meaning. God made him who knew no sin to become sin for us
(2 Corinthians 5:21). That somehow God could assume the
sting of our neglect and abuse then love us there, in a manner
that corresponds with a parent's love but transcends it, brought
hope for healing. Might we begin to believe that the Father can
fill our gaps with holy love? That hope requires the marvel of
resurrection. Having considered the cross as the distance between Parent/Child, the resurrection manifests the bond of su-

preme union between Father and Son. Jesus broke the veil of sin in all its depth and complexity and arose back into unfettered union with the Father.

HOPE FOR REUNION

Resurrection means the full bridging of that gap. God and God eclipse suffering with intimacy. Their wound is bound up in healing. The two are reunited—the tearing between Father and Son now wholly bound up in perfect love. I can only assume that the agony of sin's separation is superseded by a joy and delight in the Other's presence that has no bounds. That love leaps the boundaries of their relationship and invites us to share in their joy.

In that way, Father and Son include us in their reunion. We too can share in their victory, their healing, as Jesus invites us as human sons and daughters back into communion with his Father. We thus become partakers of his resurrection—the Father/Son reunion. With the Son, we can go directly to the Father. Love frees us from "the empty way of life handed down to [us] by [our] forefathers" (1 Peter 1:18). Formerly enslaved to the powers and traditions of this world due to the gaps in our lives, Jesus liberates us to be one with the Father, with full rights and privileges as his sons and daughters. "You are no longer a slave, but a son" (Galatians 4:7).

Resurrection means the power to become solid and secure in the love of the Father. Standing before him through the marvel of the cross, we awaken to his loving attentiveness, his affirmation and his tender affection toward us. His love is like a mother's and a father's and yet vastly superior; he supersedes them both. His love pours like precious metal into the foundation of our houses. His way solidifies in us. Love becomes the anchor of our houses, firm and secure (Hebrews 6:19). We need both trustworthy men and women in his body to administer aspects of that love. We can receive those offerings freely when we realize they make known the real love of the Father. Through repeatedly engaging with these sources of love, the Father solidifies his love in us, and makes it the bedrock of our humanity.

During our time in their city, both male and female prayer healers laid hands on Carmen and Fernando. They took time to simply abide with each of them, listening to the Father and to the couple as to the specific needs arising in them. That was crucial. Once some of their gaps were exposed, Carmen and Fernando needed tenderness and empowerment. They needed the healing presence of God. That presence is nothing less than the Spirit of the Father and Son, a spiritual love made tangible through the Body of Christ.

Healing prayer frees us to receive the "love that surpasses knowledge" (Ephesians 3:19). Though an imperfect conduit, inspired prayer has power to manifest Perfection himself. He in turn establishes us in his love all the more—one encounter, one glimpse, one prayer at a time.

BONDING WITH THE TENDER FATHER

Carmen became aware of how the quiet bond of despair with her mother made it difficult to simply be before the Lord and receive his tenderness toward her. Stillness brought up the threat of her mother's greater need, and her devices to manipulate Carmen into meeting that need. Carmen lost the freedom to need a mother's love. She had a huge need for tenderness and consolation yet barely knew it. When she discovered that God could love her like a mother does, she began to weep. A female team member prayed for her and released a river of mercy into the desert of Carmen's contained inner world. The pray-er's presence mediated the presence of the

Father for her, freeing her to receive from him at the level she so desperately needed.

Something similar happened to Fernando. Memories of his mother were pleasant but vague. All he had was a dull ache for her. During the same teaching that touched Carmen, he began to discover his need for the Father's maternal love. Once he began to receive that love, the Holy Spirit brought up grief. What was dull emotionally became acute, and he wept like a baby. All the more did Fernando need the love that surpasses mere knowledge. Through Christ's Body, the Father gave it to him abundantly that day.

These words from Isaiah ministered deeply to both: "Shout for joy, O heavens; rejoice, O earth; burst into song, O mountains! For the LORD comforts his people and will have compassion on his afflicted ones. But Zion said, 'The LORD has forsaken me; the Lord has forgotten me.' Can a mother forget the baby at her breast and have no compassion on the child she has borne? Though she may forget, I will not forget you! See, I have engraved you on the palms of my hands; your walls are ever before me" (Isaiah 49:13-16).

MAKING PEACE WITH THE FATHER'S STRONG LOVE

Both Carmen and Fernando had a harder time welcoming the more masculine dimension of the Father's love. Each faced unique wounds from their natural fathers. For Carmen, *father* meant a male face that disappears and causes pain in his absence; for Fernando, *father* meant an arbitrary presence that often demanded more than Fernando could deliver. Yet both wanted to trust their heavenly Father. Carmen knew that her containment toward Fernando and to some extent God was bound up in detachment from her father. And Fernando knew that he needed more power with which to love her boldly—to press into the distance that was beginning to define their marriage.

Male team members prayed for both of them, that they might be able to receive and contain the holy love of the Father. Both knew that they needed to be empowered in their inner selves by God's unfailing love, and so overcome the threat of bad fathering. It helped them to know that their heavenly Father used his power to fight for them, not against them. He went the distance for them; he employed his strength to draw near to them to win them in love.

These words from Moses helped them: "The LORD your God, who is going before you, will fight for you, as he did for you in Egypt, before your very eyes, and in the desert. There you saw how the LORD your God carried you, as a father carries his son, all the way you went until you reached this place" (Deuteronomy 1:30-31).

"As a father carries a child . . . until you reached this place." Both began to receive that love as central to their histories—an awesome yet deeply personal strength that had sustained them up until this point. They received afresh the truth that God was intent on making himself known to each as the Father who would not fail them. Both received the assurance that the Father would help them to rise up and fight for the truth—in their case, the truth of their marriage and young family.

God quickened his full love in Carmen and Fernando over those days. He shored up their foundations in love. He revealed himself as the One who was equal parts strength and benevolence, as mighty as he was nurturing. He manifested himself to them as the perfect parent who had and who would love them all the days of their lives. That love began to expose and loosen some of the childish expectations they still held toward their parents. Adult children cannot insist that parents acknowledge and repair the neglect or abuse of the past. That relieved Carmen and Fernando.

Holy love opens doors and windows of grace that free us to begin to see the truth: even the most earnest parents are not able to establish us wholly in love. That requires Father and Son acting marvelously on our behalf through the Holy Spirit.

That love takes time to solidify. Here the cross conveys the power of that love over and over—in an instant, it manifests to our fragile hearts the tearing (crucifixion) and the reunion (resurrection) between Father and Son. We feel many things, and are tempted by familiar strongholds of thought and emotion that appear to be our most fundamental reality. Deeper still is the unchanging work of the cross. Calvary is a fortress that the Spirit makes blessedly fluid as its meaning descends into our depths and anchors us in love.

Our gaps assumed in that marvelous gap between Father and Son, we join with Jesus in unfettered intimacy with our good Father. The cross activates that rhythm over and over; the Body of Christ mediates that rhythm, and love becomes the foundation of our lives.

God increased that foundational work in Carmen and Fernando over our days together. It is a process of healing that continues in their lives to this day, especially through good friends with whom they continue to pray for these foundational realities.

God has great things in store for all of our "houses." The cross atop the house bears witness to the unfailing love at the base—the ground on which we can love others well.

4

OPENING DOORS

THE RIGOROUS BEAUTY
OF ROMANTIC LOVE

I slept, but my heart was awake.

   Listen! My lover is knocking:

"Open to me, my sister, my darling,

   my dove, my flawless one." . . .

My lover thrust his hand through the latch-opening;

   my heart began to pound for him.

SONG OF SOLOMON 5:2, 4

Nobody should seek his own good, but the good of others.

1 CORINTHIANS 10:24

The foundation of any sound temple is love. The deeper and stronger that love is, the more enduring will be the love offered to others. Jesus seeks to establish us in love; he wants to make it solid in us. He wills for love to become the base of each Christian "home." That love is as tender as it is strong. Born of God and relayed from faithful ones who love us well, love is gold. It establishes our value.

And love frees us to value others. When we are treated as valuable, we ascribe value to others. Love lays its girders deep within us; on love we stand and endure what we must in order for love to mature in us and become our main offering to others. Carmen and Fernando loved each other as best they could for as long as they could. Without the greater love breaking in through Jesus and his Body, their weak love for each other could have died—another divorce, another child shuttled from broken parent to broken parent. Love had a better plan.

THE SPIRIT OF SELF-GIVING

Love beckons to us constantly, urging us to go the distance. The Spirit of Jesus and the Father urges us to go the distance. The Spirit sustained both in the darkness of crucifixion then reunited them. That very Spirit lives in us, imploring us to go the distance in love. That Spirit is love. God gave all. God gives all to us. His essence? Self-giving.

His surrender at Calvary was an offering for us. For the sake of making us his own. He agonized for us because he ascribes value to us. He ascribes value to all. He gives each Christian that Spirit of self-giving and endurance. And he commissions each of us according to that Spirit to make every effort to ascribe value to one another. He frees us to recognize our need for love, but to not allow our needs to prevail when another's is greater. I see this constantly in friendship, in marriage, in parenting. Love frees us to behold the other and to seek to love him or her by putting his or her need for love above our own.

Love not only lays girders in us, it washes our windows and cleans the air so that we can see the other rightly. When Annette and I first married we lived in seminary housing in Pasadena, a smoggy (and otherwise stunning) town just east of downtown Los Angeles. We were told that our apartment, perched on the edge of a freeway, was just a mile or two from a beautiful mountain range. We could not see it through the haze.

In the heat and pressure of seminary and ministry, we newlyweds often failed to see the other—the beauty and neediness of two weak human beings. But in blessed moments, I would behold Annette as she is—radiant, tender, passionate, full of need and virtue. I would see her in her genuine loveliness. I would catch the nuance of what she wanted but would not demand, and I would want more than anything to meet that need—to satisfy her because I valued her.

In so doing, my masculinity was activated. The Spirit of Jesus arose in me and strengthened my offering to her. I stood on the solid ground of love and loved. The winds blew and the rain fell, and I was freed to see the one to whom God had entrusted me. The magnificence of her design, like the purple hills now visible across the freeway, engendered awe and gratitude to the Designer himself. He freed me to see then, and to continue to see thirty years later, a vision of beauty that I could otherwise lose sight of in the haze of a cluttered life.

I don't adapt well to prescribed ideas of romance. For example, Annette and I tend not to be overly romantic on Valentine's Day. Too much chocolate and champagne and exposure to dippy romantic comedies makes me alternately dull and hostile—an anti-romantic. But the call of the divine Spirit to stand my ground of love and to behold and bless what is truly lovely— that is living. The love of Christ awakens "the deepest and most real possibilities and dispositions of our humanity"; he trains us to manifest those possibilities, to realize them by becoming a people who truly, genuinely, actually value others because they are worthy of value.

In that way, we prepare for the rigors of romance; divine love frees us to find and stand our ground—the solid base of love. We need love's solidity on what can be the shifting sand and confusing signposts of our longings for love.

I am not only referring to married people here. I know amazing singles who are alive to their sexuality yet without partnership. Though alone, they are not dominated by their loneliness. One blessed friend in Portland, Oregon, stands out—she resides in a beautiful home full of color and creativity that has become a source of life for many. Whenever she invites me and others into her home, we leave full of life. She engenders new life out of the temple God has entrusted to her. As fully and as freely as she dares, she gives herself to others with need and candor and gifts expressed in a generous spirit.

An elder in her own church, she in her home reminds me of a little church. Whenever we meet there, we "are being built together to become a dwelling in which God lives by his Spirit." She is smart and verbal—she speaks "the truth in love" there, so that all who hear can better "grow up into him who is the Head, that is, Christ." In her home, we as friends and fellow believers grow and build each other up in love, "as each part does its work." Together we rise and "become a holy temple in the Lord," better together than apart to know him through our love for one another (Ephesians 2:22; 4:15-16; 2:21).

Love that values others and thus engenders new life is God's call upon all believers, single and married. It is the base on which we stand and see the good gifts around us. From that base we learn how to offer ourselves wisely and well so we can do our part to grow together as "a living temple." In that way we manifest Christ—we make him known to one another and to the world around us. Together we aspire to him, through his grace. Together we enter fully into life—a living temple.

EMBRACING GENDER WHOLENESS

Who we are for each other as gender opposites plays a key role in our lives together. We must each answer the question: Who will man be for woman and who will woman be for man? Not only will our answer help determine our community and our creativity—it is key in making known God's ultimate plan for all of humanity.

Think about it. The Bible begins with a beautiful but fractured love story between a man and a woman. Adam and Eve—the original bridegroom and bride—become one then mess up badly. Cast out from the garden, they blaze a trail of sexual and gender brokenness until God manifests himself in Jesus, the Bridegroom, who gave all in order to reclaim broken ones and make them his own. That gathering of being-healed-ones is nothing less than his bride, the aforementioned "living temple," his church. The Bible ends with the promise that this being-healed-bride will be made pure and holy and ready to receive Jesus in full. She will be made ready to consummate union with him. As theologian Christopher West says beautifully, "The whole story of our salvation is contained between the love of the Bridegroom and the Bride. These nuptial bookends are key to interpreting all that lies between them."

Gender is holy. Man and woman together reflect an aspect of who God is. He created humanity in his image as male and female (Genesis 1:26-27). We possess authority to make him known—to represent him—in how we care for members of the opposite gender. It may or may not involve sexual love. All are under the divine command to aspire to harmony between man and woman. That harmony—a rightful reliance upon the other in his or her difference from oneself—composes gender wholeness. It is holy.

Maybe that has something to do with the creative and yet the crucifying nature of gender difference. We are drawn to each other. Otherness attracts. For most, the appeal of the other is somehow based on what the other possesses that we know only in part. The other is mysterious, fully human but "other." The lure of his or her difference draws us in. We are attracted to what we long for and yet barely know. And opposites annoy us. The charm and lure of his or her difference just as readily becomes a threat to our sanity. We ask ourselves, *Is that really a good way of thinking or feeling? Isn't my way better, more real, more human?*

Up close and personal, gender differences test the quality of our love. They crucify any illusion of our selflessness. Once the other's charm and our own sensual curiosity subside, we may be left with little more than judgments about the other's limits. The "whole image"—humanity as male and female—reveals our brokenness. In the glare of the "other," we behold our chronic self-seeking.

WHOLLY "OTHER" AND THE HOLY OTHER

Perhaps God's plan in the dance of gender difference is to not only rouse us but also to crucify us. For he too is "Other." He is the Holy God. He is the Creator, we are the created. He is far beyond our knowing, and what we do know about him is only through his accommodation to our small size and dim minds. He is the ultimate "Other." And he will not tolerate us making him in our image as if we were the Creator, and he the object of our design. "You turn things upside down, as if the potter were thought to be like the clay! Shall what is formed say to him who formed it, 'he did not make me'? Can the pot say of the potter, 'he knows nothing'?" (Isaiah 29:16).

Here we begin to see the link between God's will for our spirituality and for our relationships. He wants to make us good through revealing the limits of our love; he then subordinates us to those relationships in which we will grow in love. We bear his image well when we offer ourselves to him and others in the arduous task of learning to love well. Mike Mason in his excellent book *The Mystery of Marriage* writes: "Our natural tendency is to treat people as if they were not 'others' at all but mere aspects of ourselves . . . and incidentally, that is also what true religion is supposed to do—to remind us that God is not an idol, a human invention, not an extension or projection of ourselves."

God is holy—he is the Ultimate Other. He commands that we love him wholly. And he employs the opposite gender as a little "other" to teach us to love others well. In that way, we fulfill the two great commands: loving God and loving others (Matthew 22:38-40). Mason is wise to compare our relationship with God as "holy other" with his call to represent him clearly and humbly in the challenge of gender difference. "Both deal in the most direct way possible with the phenomenon of otherness in our lives, with relationship. Both feed on our sense of encounter with someone who is like us, resembling us in image, but not us."

Here we discover our need for Jesus above all else. God the Holy Other has made himself known to us in the bloody and exalted Christ. We need the witness of both his glory and his wounds. Though we aspire to love well, we fail miserably. The wounds of loving poorly compete with the deeper cry of our hearts to break out of fear and isolation and into holy communion.

That is where he wants us. Perhaps that is the convergence of holy longing and frustration where he seeks to do his deepest work in us. Jesus helps us in our weakness. In our quest to both honor him and make him known in how we love, we need Jesus more and more. I am amazed at how Jesus blesses my aspirations to love by drawing me to himself, over and over again.

Annette and I recently shared a vacation together. Rare—no kids. We both expected much time in which to enjoy one another, a second honeymoon, if you will. Sadly, Annette hurt her back just before embarking on our thousand-mile journey. She was not a happy camper. By the time we arrived at our destination, she was in agony. We spent most of the time looking for medical help and trying to get Annette as comfortable as possible. Annette was a great sport and I tried hard. Really I did.

Toward the end of our trip, I began to feel resentful. My hopes of a kick-off to our second honeymoon were dashed. Chiropractics marked our "empty nest" more than sexual gymnastics. I thought I was concealing my distress. Wrong. My sexuality seemed to be spilling out all over the place. Annette commented on how unusually attentive I was to our server at the restaurant and wondered if I were flirting. Flirting? I was aghast. And busted.

I actually felt entitled to something, somewhere, from someone. I was mad. I stammered that she may be right but then lit into her about some things I had stored up over the last few weeks. I felt justified. I was tipping the scales of injustice—the terrible tragedy that I simply had to give a little more to Annette in these days than I wanted. Her distress required that I give more to her than I was accustomed, and I did not like it.

She started crying and blurted out that she feels she can never go for long with having greater need than I have. She was right, and we drove home the last leg of the trip barely speaking to each other. She went to bed and I stayed up and stewed. I went out to water the plants in the hot August night. For some reason, the hose got tangled up and barely any water came out. In fact all I ended up doing was watering the dirt on the porch floor.

I made mud: a fitting metaphor to the mess I had made of our second honeymoon.

I stayed up and prayed. One thing I know about my bad behavior: Only One can bear it. Only the mercy of Jesus Christ can wash away my sin and shame. Only his real presence can make my heart tender unto repentance. What really impacted me in this prayer time was the conviction of how much I had wounded Annette. I was reminded of how much she needs me to bear with her in her greater need.

Why? Because she has intrinsic value and is worthy of my attention. Before God, that is the truth. Regardless of any distraction, or need, or sense of entitlement on my part, she is worthy of my love in whatever way it is right and appropriate for me to give it. Freed from shame, I was ready to repent before her and make amends. I went to bed where she was still stirring and we talked and prayed long into the night. Soon after, a typical summer storm roared through Kansas City. It watered the plants and washed away the mud on the porch. It seemed to make all things new again. Just like the mercy of God. He reveals the truth of sin in order to cleanse and reinvigorate the love he wills for us to extend to one another.

AVOIDING LOVE

Often when I share with other Christians about this call to love the opposite gender boldly and heartily, they squirm.

Are we more comfortable in our contained worlds of spiritual ideals, or in the high octane worlds of promiscuity? Christopher West refers to these two extremes as angelism or animalism.

Angelism involves the tendency to refuse to offer oneself to others out of fear of the other and one's own body. Here one is apt to spiritualize the detachment as if one were being more faithful to God in keeping a safe distance from the other.

Remember my teammate friend Lucy? She fit snugly into that "detachment" category. She feared rejection and at the same time agreed with those men who had rejected her. She felt unworthy of love and attention and so she rejected men before they could reject her. She refused to value men for fear that they might devalue her were she to subject herself to them. Thinking herself pure and holy, she was just defending herself from the threat of rejection.

Carmen and Fernando were not much different. They struggled to tell the truth to each other. They were more comfortable in their containment—in passively acquiescing to spiritual ideals of love and faithfulness. They needed to break the silence—to ascribe value to the other and at the same time to give voice to their need for each other.

Rick is the one who loved the concept of a woman more than a real one. He volleyed between same-sex attraction and fantasies of the perfect woman who would complete him. Yet he remained aloof from most women on the grounds of their imperfection. Rick had yet to love a real woman, one whose beauty matched her flaws. He had yet to discover the power of love to activate his own sexuality. His house was not yet ready to forsake illusion and discover the "otherness" of real flesh-and-blood females.

Animalism is the other extreme that marks our inability to truly love the "other." Here we become bound by broken patterns of relating that set us adrift in currents of sensual and emotional addictions. We objectify others here, making them something they are not—the fantasy completion of our own damaged, unformed selves.

My teammate Jake had done this most of his life. Women were conquests to him. He could seduce them but could not love them for who they actually were. Valuing only their sensuality, he actually devalued women. He admitted: "Once I have them, I don't really want them. It's all in the dance. Then when it's over, I move on. After the rush or conquest, whatever you want to call it, I feel empty. Then it's just a matter of time before I move on."

Bev had been subject to the animalism of her uncle's sexual abuse of her. As such, she had sought refuge in a string of highly dependent (and short-lived) relationships with women. In romancing the same gender, she only prolonged her own refusal to face the pain of her life, and from facing men as they are—not mere abusers but real people as capable of love as she was.

Angelism and animalism are often two sides of the same person. The pious and detached believer, reacting to the threat of sin, can readily digress into more veiled forms of sin in vulnerable moments. For example, both Rick and Fernando prided themselves on their spirituality and yet failed more than not to stay away from Internet porn. Lucy struggled with extended bouts of romantic fantasy. And though Bev hated the effects of sexual abuse, she also hated the lustful aspects of her lesbian unions.

Their stories make it clear: we cannot avoid or deny the divine command to love the other heartily and boldly. For this we must once again take up the call to love the other because they are worthy of our offering.

A wise woman writes: "Living with such beauty and blemish, we are not to find an excuse to escape either by sinning boldly or dancing above the stars. The more difficult venture to which we are called is to love carefully and patiently." And I dare add, boldly! Toward that end, we need a way forward.

The way is simple yet arduous—we must commit ourselves to the good of another rather than making that commitment hinge upon the goods we get from him or her. Only in valuing that person as an end in him- or herself can we sustain a stable relationship.

That selfless approach to love was expounded upon by Karol Wojtyla decades before he became Pope John Paul II. He claims that we as God's image-bearers are unique in our capacity to be aware of the good that another needs and that we are able to act on that good—to seek that good for another. What sets us apart from the rest of creation is that we can think about another's good and choose to act on that good. Yet we are also creatures full of need and desire whose heads and hearts are readily turned by the sheer attraction we feel toward some and not others.

VALUING THE PERSON

That is where the rigor of genuine relating comes in. Desire alone is not enough. We must always aspire to value the person rather than the pleasure we derive from that person. Love must subordinate desire. Though it is human and normal to long for particular ones, those longings alone are not the mark of our Christian humanity. One inspired mark of the Christian is the commitment to long for what is best for another.

That is a challenge. How many times have we heard of a marriage dashed on the rocks by one party falling out of love with one partner and into love with another? Or the single person dating one person after another in a fog of need and desire? How about the one who withholds love for fear of not being able to deliver love as the other needs?

To live as a true image-bearer is awesome. It should provoke holy fear in us. Any who have been abused or betrayed bear the mark of those who chose neither to see nor act upon the good of another. Woe to those who cause Christ's little ones to stumble! It would be better for them to be thrown into the sea with a millstone tied around their necks (Luke 17:2). It is fearsome to stand in the dignity of what it means to be an image-bearer: to love another based on what is best for him/her rather than on what immediately pleases oneself. We are all familiar with our native neediness, how motivated we are by physical longings or sentimental ideals. Yet how much more noble are they who act according to the value of another, regardless of what it costs them?

Bev began to reckon with this question of value, what was actually best for another. Though she felt a form of love for her female partners, she knew that they were based more on mutual need and brokenness than on mature self-giving. Her love issued more out of what she was getting rather than out of what she could freely give; in that way, she knew that she stood in the way between Christ and her friends. Her emotional and sexual entanglements muddied her capacity to be clear agents of Jesus for them.

She left her last relationship for the sake of love, love as Jesus defines it. In her absence, Bev gave God room to act in her life and in the other's. In that way she demonstrated that she valued what was best for another over her own needs. Surrendering a lover for the sake of the Gospel may just be a fulfillment of what it means to lose one's life for the sake of finding it in Christ alone.

Fernando and Carmen faced a different challenge. Both were subject to different sets of expectations of the other in that season of marriage. Both of these sets of ideals had to be laid down for the greater call to value the other. Why? Simply because the other is worthy of value.

Carmen had been drawn to Fernando for his kindness and

tenderness toward her. She idealized him in a way, and loved the idea of him as an exemplary Christian husband and father. A different season of challenges caused her to see him in a new light. Not only was he not the ideal, he was weak and ineffectual, a shadow of the ideal she had bonded with early on. This discrepancy between the ideal and the real tempted her to hate him where she had once loved him.

Fernando had loved Carmen for her physical attractiveness and also her limited need of himself. In her containment, she was beautiful to him. He could partake of her beauty physically; that satisfied him and kept him engaged with her sensually. Childbirth changed things. Carmen was neither as physically attractive nor sexually available to him. Instead she seemed cold and demanding, not the ideal he recalled. At times he felt contempt for her, an emotion that frightened the normally mild man.

Love had to become greater than the ideals at hand. Carmen needed Fernando to be stronger than he was; he needed her to be sexually available and yet noble. Each had to find the greater power to act as Christians—to love the other because the other is worthy of that love, not because the other satisfied a certain ideal.

The key here was for both to see what was going on and to commit themselves to Jesus as the basis for a higher love. Both needed the healing community to do so. They partook of Living Waters, which renewed their desire and capacity to be good gifts to each other. Together in large group discussion and healing, then separately in the same-sex small group, they came to understand how Jesus was refining their love for each other— burning off ideals and helping them to commit themselves squarely to the realities at hand.

They began to fulfill this truth in their marriage with the

help of Jesus and his community: "The correct gravitational pull that enables sentiment and attraction to become love is the value of the person as a person. When love is based merely on sexual attraction or emotional fulfillment, the decisive feature is what I am getting out of the relationship—what stirs me—rather than the inherent value of the person."

Jesus was maturing them in love. Not content for them to take a poetic leap over the reality of the one they married, Jesus used a new season of their life together to reveal the complex reality of the lover at hand. Jesus was not content for them to use the other merely as an opportunity for one's own purpose or desire. He was calling them to value the other, to accord what was best for him or her, not for oneself.

For Fernando, that meant loving Carmen—reaching out to her, showing her love and affection because she needed it, not because it meant the promise of sex. And for Carmen, it meant appreciating what Fernando could give her. She also learned to verbalize what she was going through in this season and to bless Fernando for the ways he could help her. Both made an effort to show the other value and dignity.

"The command to love forces one to see the other as truly other than the self, when what we so often attempt in love is to see the other as an extension of one's wishes and desires." Jesus turns our ideals into reality as we submit our loves to him. We arise out of a misty idealism and into one who can see another as that person is and ascribe value to him or her. That clear seeing and action composes the truest dimensions of what it means to bear God's image—to represent him well on the earth.

LOVE AGES WELL

Seeing others as they are is the best soil for bringing new life on earth. I am only grateful for my amazing parents who, after almost sixty years of marriage, continue to value one another. Throughout their life together, they have sought to show dignity to each other. In good and troubled seasons, I have never witnessed them dehumanizing the other.

I have had the privilege of spending time with both in their home of late. Now in their eighties, I witness the power of their tender and practical care for each other. I know I am blessed by the witness of these two amazing image-bearers. I am an heir to the dignity and value they have ascribed to each other. As they have fulfilled these words through the witness of their lives together, so will I aspire to do the same toward Annette:

> Love is put to the test when the sensual and emotional attractions weaken . . . nothing then remains but the value of the person, and the inner truth about the love of those concerned comes to light. If their love is a true gift of the self, it will not only survive but will grow stronger and sink deeper roots.

God is merciful to us. He does not commission us to sink roots into relationships that we are not yet ready to invest in. He cares for the well-being of others, and does not will for them to be damaged by our fledging efforts at love. So he prepares us according to what we can handle, and what is appropriate for another to bear. He wants all to arise out of immaturity and into real love for others based on their inherent value.

PEOPLE BEFORE PLEASURE OR POWER

Jake, for example, was not ready to date a woman. He needed first to understand that a woman was a person, not merely the sum of her sexual parts or a conquest that demonstrated his power over her. It was honestly difficult for him to turn down the erotic, romantic component of relating to woman; he could not do it at first. But in the humility inspired by spiritual discipline, he began to have ears to hear and eyes to see.

The most powerful tool for awakening his conscience was the truth of the pain he had caused others. Part of his discipline involved a controlled opportunity for him to listen to the painful confession of several women whom he had used for sex. For the first time, he heard their confusion, disorientation, even their loss of faith in reaction to how he abused his spiritual position to get what he wanted. At first, these women did not know that there had been many others. They needed to tell the truth of what it is like for a woman to be discarded and replaced—to be treated as a disposable item. And Jake needed to hear that truth.

"At first I could barely hear it: tears, anger, even rage. They seemed so different than when we were first together. They had been so fun, so open. I thought: 'Who are they talking about?' Then I began to realize that was me—I did that, I caused that kind of damage. I was clueless. And I feel like I am still waking up to what I did," he confessed.

His lack of self-control had resulted in cruelty—violence to the souls and bodies of others. But the truth was beginning to set him free. Jake opened his heart to change. God began to transform his approach to erotic and romantic love into a matter of conscience. How? By facing the damage he had done. Then, by God's grace, Jake began to discover that these "bodies" were actually people of value.

It took time for Jake to begin to relate to women as whole persons. He needed boundaries that clearly defined women as friends, not intimates. With those boundaries intact, he began to work on demonstrating the sacrificial love that esteems women because they are people of value, not mere bodies.

VALUABLE OFFERING

God is gracious in that process of learning to love the opposite
gender as people, not stereotypes of desire or of derision. Lucy
tended more toward the latter. She needed men and resisted
them at the same time. She was finding her voice in relation to
them. But more than that, she needed solid opposite-sex friendships with whom she could grow. Her commitment? To show
them value as people.

She actually had little experience with men. In some ways,
she had used her tongue to distance herself from the threat of
rejection. So she aimed to find a couple of guys with whom she
could just be friends and make an effort to know and value
them. That way, the relationship could result in another being
blessed and built up. She would grow in a kind of sacrificial
giving, and all involved might be that much better able to care
for and trust members of the opposite sex.

She chose a couple of guys who loved Jesus—one at work and
another at church—who were at different places entirely with
women. One had just come off a bad dating relationship, the
other was awkward and clearly nervous about relating to women
at all. Lucy began to relate to them as people, neither potential
rejecters nor life partners. It made a huge difference to unhook
from the threat of either extreme and to simply value them and
to discover who they were as human beings. She realized that
she had power in God to do so. She was not subject to them as
the weaker feminine party; she was subject to God to show them
value, and they were subject to each other before God.

PREPARING TO VALUE THE OTHER

For both Rick and Bev, opposite-sex romance was not the first
priority. Both needed to focus on other things: Bev on the healing of sexual abuse, and Rick on overcoming the illusions he

held toward the opposite sex. Though he had no history of violating women per se, he needed to grow up and learn to address women as women, not illusions of perfection. Both needed to face more seriously the gender brokenness related to same-sex attraction.

Fernando and Carmen were, you could say, nearer than the others to exercising sacrificial love to each other. But all of our friends faced the same challenge. Each lived under the divine command to extend value to the "other" as an expression of what it means to bear the image of God. Each lived under Paul's command, in fear and trembling, to "submit to one another out of reverence for Christ" (Ephesians 5:21).

I say fear and trembling because it is no small thing to live as the created, saved by the grace of Jesus, and yet be called to love as he loves. As we make that commitment to love our neighbor as ourselves, and apply that command to our romantic, sexual lives, we are subject to serious conviction. How far we have fallen from being Jesus to one another!

In truth, we in these temples are far more subject to devaluing the other and defending ourselves, more inclined to taking advantage of the other or nourishing petty offenses. We love poorly at best. Especially when seen under the spotlight of our preeminent image-bearer—Christ himself. Before his awesome faithfulness, we all must admit our unfaithfulness.

This quote jumped off the page at me: "Love demands of each individual Christian the disturbing acknowledgement that we do not in the least know how to love faithfully." Our gender and sexual selves, full of spiritual meaning and earthy longings, must ultimately answer these questions: "How well have I loved?" "Have I ascribed value to those around me because they are valuable, not because of my gain in doing so?"

Unlike the pop culture that insists on personal satisfaction above all else, especially in the sexual and emotional realms, Jesus commands another standard. He commands that we love our neighbor as ourselves. And the whole of scripture points to the relationship between male and female as the content of that greatest commandment.

Marriage does not fulfill that command, as if Fernando and Carmen had realized "love" simply by being married. Not at all! Marriage has served a marvelous crucifying purpose in their lives—to highlight how they have not loved in order to make more room for his grace. He uses marriage to expose our illusions about love. Jesus uses the mirror of the other to expose our cruelties, our illusions, and our petty self-concerns. In so doing, he reduces us to love.

REDUCED TO GRACE

Jesus is the answer. And the challenge. He is our source of compassion when we submit to the crushing requirement of his call to love this other as he would have us love him or her. Subject to the call, we fall forward into his grace. That grace "is our only possible source of hope in our blundering attempts at love." Beware of conservatives who appear righteous and yet who use their traditional guise to cover a multitude of petty and monstrous cruelties. Remember that the prostitutes are entering the kingdom of heaven before the Pharisees (Matthew 21:31)!

Whatever our starting point, we kneel before the same cross. We acknowledge that we are invaluable and created to engender that value in others; we live before God as those created to bear his image and represent that image well to others. In the same breath, we admit that we are yet broken and cruel in our lovelessness. As priests and prostitutes, the traditional and perverse, both chaste and addicted, we enter into the same pool of mercy, aware of both the crushing requirement to love well and the grace that will enable us to do so.

In a culture that seems like a "freeway" of romantic and erotic love, we take up our crosses. We as Christians embrace the countercultural call of Jesus to love sacrificially in our sexual and gender selves. The words of Kierkegaard speak into the cultural void far better than I can. His grasp of true Christian love pierces the darkness of our culture of entitlement, especially in the sexual and gender realms. Speaking of the church in his day, he says: "It is all love and love . . . because God is Love and Love—nothing at all about rigorousness must be heard; it must all be the free language and nature of love. . . . God's love easily becomes a fabulous and childish conception, the figure of Christ too mild and sickly-sweet for it to be true that Jesus was and is an offense."

Jesus' love offends us in order to free us to love other bodies as persons created in God's image. That is a non-negotiable mandate for any who take Jesus seriously. The rigor of his command to love well, coupled with the grace that forgives our failures to do so, frames the door of our house. We proceed out expectantly and soberly in offering ourselves to others in love.

5

HOUSING DESIRE

LIMITS THAT LIBERATE

She watches over the affairs of her household.

PROVERBS 31:27

"And I myself will be a wall of fire around it," declares the LORD,

"and I will be its glory within."

ZECHARIAH 2:5

Sexual longing, when motivated by the desire to value another human being, brings out the best in both genders. A man manifests his masculinity when he blesses a woman out of both respect and desire; the woman who responds to him possesses an enhanced beauty. Secure and confirmed in love, she blesses him and confirms the goodness of his offering to her.

I have the privilege to witness this awakening of true desire in those who come out of a history of sexual brokenness, including same-sex attraction. These ones have labored long in the belief that they were somehow disqualified from the "dance" between man and woman. Then, in God's steady redemptive work, one begins to see the other gender with new eyes. Extraordinary in its purity, the one perceives the "other" for the first time—not as best friend or abuser or besides-the-point, but as a counterpart, created by God, desirable, worthy of being pursued and blessed.

A GOOD GIFT

These desires begin only as a trickle and build as one makes the effort to position oneself as a gift that wants to give itself out of sheer longing to please the other. When I saw Rick and Lucy again after a few months, I could scarcely believe what I saw. Something had awakened in Rick. He had begun purposefully to relate to a woman a few weeks earlier. For the first time, he was motivated to reach beyond himself and his own gender to bless her. He felt new emotions and desires; his ardor enhanced his manhood.

Lucy admitted to me shyly that one of her male friendships had intensified. She carefully referred to him as a friend. But I could tell in her eyes and in the glow of her skin that she loved this man's attentiveness to her. She loved it as much as she feared it. She feared another failure, the threat that a good offering that gave her life and hope could also be withheld, and only enhance her loneliness.

I overheard the two giving each other little pep talks—Lucy urging Rick to take it slow and treat her with respect so that a friendship can endure even if romance doesn't, Rick reminding Lucy that she is a beautiful girl and a good gift: "the guy's just lucky to know you, Lucy!" I was really blessed by that. These were two people of the opposite sex who knew how to bless and build up each other. I hoped that they would enjoy their new friendships as much as they enjoyed each other, to take delight in the "dance" without undue weightiness.

I love to witness the beauty and purity of human sexuality in opposite-sex friendship. I marvel at it. It sings God's song to me, how he woos us with such tenderness and kindness and makes us beautiful in our response to him.

The other day at the airport I witnessed two college students saying good-bye, presumably for a long time, if the amount of tears and kisses and dorky parting gifts were any indication. They were unadorned in their care for each other, sweetly unsophisticated and thus that much more enlivened by the other, unreserved in sentiment and touch. They cared nothing about who knew. Artless and yet full of the Creator's design: male ardor awakening the beauty of a woman's response who in turn blesses the man—nothing more exquisite and creative. For a few random moments, I celebrated with them how God meets his creatures in loneliness and provides what we need as we give ourselves to the loveliness of the other.

He is in it all, especially when we know him by name. Then even the challenges of love can be redeemed because he is there, working all for the good. I recall one afternoon in our dating season when I surprised Annette at her apartment. She did not answer her door, yet I knew she was inside so I slowly made my way in. She sat alone in a chair, no make-up, a tear-stained face, looking blankly out the opposite window. She was depressed, a state that would come over her on occasion, due to some significant unhealed wounding as a child.

I wanted to run. This wasn't the buoyant woman I was dating! For a moment I flashed on the experience of a few weeks before when Annette received some powerful, Holy Spirit-inspired healing from a few girlfriends. She was filled with something glorious when I saw her next. She looked more lovely than ever to me, and I rejoiced. That's who I wanted, not the woman sitting before me in shadows.

I realized then that I had been running all my young adult life, looking for beauty without cost, seeking the confirmation of my value without actually valuing another. My eyes were open to see Annette as the sum of many things: inspiration and sorrow, engaging and detached, desirable and perplexing. And I wanted to love her. That choice to love and value her—not only in the bloom of spring, but in shadow, made all the difference.

My masculine ardor became fortified by the choice to value her because she is worthy of it. That is how God matured me. Not primarily through ministry, but through loving another in sun and storm. God strengthened me to do so; Annette grew more beautiful in my eyes as a result. Thirty years later, I desire no other partner. Holy love set a precedent for loving within the limits of what conveys value to the other. That limit liberated both of us to rejoice in the humanity—our own and the other's—that he entrusted to us.

FREEDOM OF CHOICE

One thing about desire: we have choice. We can know what is good and act upon that good in relation to this "other." That choice liberates us to grow in love. To choose well, we must first be united with Christ. That seems perfectly reasonable but must be reiterated over and over. Unless and until our first choice is Jesus, we can be deceived by the power of desire and make choices that devalue others.

I see it like this. We each are a house that possesses doors that open both ways. We have authority to be our own gate-keeper; we let some people and things in and keep others out. We make decisions constantly about these "ins and outs." And we are vulnerable to poor decisions. That is especially true at the level of our sexuality—our longing to draw near to some houses and not others, the loneliness that at times aches to be eased, the worldly illusions that set us up for deception.

The power of sexual and romantic longing can readily intoxicate us gatekeepers. We then can sicken ourselves and sometimes others. Whereas whole sexual relating can be a revelation of masculine strength and feminine beauty, broken sexuality hurts humanity and makes it unholy. Maybe that is what Paul warned us about in 1 Corinthians 3:16-17 when he says: "Don't you know that you yourselves are God's temple and that God's Spirit lives in you? If anyone destroys God's temple, God will destroy him; for God's temple is sacred, and you are that temple."

In other words, Paul reminds us that we are a holy house, indwelt by God himself. Yet we are fallible, as prone to false connections as readily as we are to true ones. Has God actually entrusted a holy house to much loved yet flawed priests like us? Why would he do that? The answer lies in Paul's words. "God's Spirit lives in you." That means we gatekeepers have a living, breathing advocate in the Holy Spirit who stands with us at the gate of our house, determining who and what can enter. God has not left us to our own devices. We are joined with holy counsel, "the Spirit of truth . . . will guide you into all truth" and "will teach you all things" (John 16:13; 14:26).

Being led by the Spirit as to the decisions we make concerning what we let in and out of our houses sounds simple. But it isn't. Living with Christ in the temple requires surrender. Unless we have "died with Christ," giving him the reins of our sexual and relational lives, we are prone to self-deception. We shall hear and see and choose what pleases us and squelch "that still small voice" that may advise otherwise. We are capable of rendering "the Spirit of truth" a figment of our imagination.

I have discovered this over and over again with Christians who love Jesus but yet love pleasures experienced outside the lines of truth and value even more. These are the ones who proclaim God's quick release from an unhappy marriage in order to wed the object of their adultery, those who trumpet "the gay self" and its relationships as inspired, or who hook up as singles because they have "needs, and God gets that." Unwilling to face their poor decisions as sin, they then seek to spiritualize them as "blessed."

How much better and harder is the one who surrenders to Jesus at the level of his or her affections, right from the start. It is a wise man or woman who acknowledges the power of sexuality to create and enhance, as well as to confuse and diminish. To surrender to Jesus there is to submit to him as the Lord of the gate and the temple. It is the beginning of "being led by the Spirit" at the level where it is most needed. Where else are we most inclined to act impulsively? Shortsightedly? To wrong a brother or sister or take advantage of him or her (1 Thessalonians 4:6)? We need to surrender to Jesus at the source of our longing for sexual and emotional completion with another.

Such surrender is a type of death. Far from an attempted murder of our sexuality, it is rather a yielding of our will concerning what we do with our sexuality. It means giving up independent views about how one intends to meet sexual "needs" and entrusting those needs to Jesus.

It is the type of self-denial that leads to life. Bonhoeffer defines self-denial as "knowing only Christ, and no longer oneself. It means seeing only Christ, who goes ahead of us, and no longer the path that is too difficult for us. Again, self-denial is saying only: He goes ahead of us; hold fast to him." That yielding applies as pointedly to the traditional sinner in a tepid marriage as it does to one's journey out of homosexuality.

I remember pointedly the day when Jesus through his Spirit asked me to give up the prospect of homosexual relationships, forever. In prayer, I saw a picture of a door that was slightly ajar. Jesus asked me to close it. I knew right away what it meant. Though I was an earnest Christian, I was still powerfully drawn to homosexuality. My temporary abstinence belied the truth that I was waiting for an idealized Christian man. God asked me that day to surrender that prospect to him. Forever. He simply asked me to close the door.

I had hoped he would make the choice easy; I wanted him to so reduce my same-sex desire that the moral choice at hand would be a breeze. Not so. He made his lordship clear enough to me and asked me to choose himself over the ideas I held about my sexual future. I surrendered that day. And have not reopened that door since.

Therein lay my capacity to follow him onto the sure ground of his will for my sexuality. I was able to be attentive to him because I had fully placed my trust in him. Jean-Pierre de Caussade writes: "It is not our business to decide what the ultimate purpose of such submission may be." It is simply our call to submit to Jesus as the Master of the house.

In our pursuit of spiritual integrity and sexual wholeness, we must each answer Oswald Chambers's question: "Am I willing to relinquish my hold on all my affections, and to be identified with the death of Christ?" Fernando faced that very question when dating Carmen. He recounted to me her prolonged uncertainty about their suitability for each other. He felt sure of his desire for her and their rightness as a couple. Yet he respected her lack of readiness. He surrendered to Jesus; he handed the limited control he held over his relational future and placed it in bigger hands. He realized rightfully that he could not make her love him! But he could surrender to Jesus at the level of his affections.

He released Carmen at the cross, and waited. He gave her grace and space. He grieved what he thought could be the loss of the relationship. He did not place his hope in the resurrection of a romance; he trusted in Christ, knowing that the new life Jesus gave him had an objective, enduring quality that romantic love did not. He settled the fact that life would go on even if the relationship did not. Yet he loved her; he could not shake that truth. He surrendered the outcome of that love and sought as best he could to show that love to Carmen while respecting her limits. She eventually responded to his love for her.

In the hard time they currently faced as a couple, I reminded him of his cross-centered history with Carmen—his genuine submission to Jesus in it, and how faithful Jesus was to bring new life out of death. How much more was he willing to be glorified in the renewal the two needed in the present!

Whether surrendering a powerfully good relationship or immoral options, our yielding to the Lord of the house makes all the difference. It takes the work on the cross—Jesus dying for our sinful independence—and applies it pointedly to those areas that we surrender to him. Without the surrender of our sexuality, you could say that the death he died is not able to achieve its full and redeeming impact upon our sexuality.

Chambers writes:

> The imperative need spiritually is to sign the death warrant of the disposition of sin, to turn all emotional impressions and intellectual beliefs into a moral verdict against . . . my claim to my right to myself. Paul says: "I have been crucified with Christ"; he does not say: "I have determined to imitate Christ" but "I have identified with him in his

death." When I come to such a moral decision and act upon it then all that Christ wrought for me on the cross is wrought in me. The free committal of myself to God gives the Holy Spirit the chance to impart to me the holiness of Jesus Christ.

Surrender to Jesus is key. That gives the Holy Spirit room to make us more fully his own. It frees us to face our longings for love, humanly speaking, before the Designer and Redeemer of those longings. Established in Love himself, we can wrestle through our desires and fears before him.

TRUSTING THE BODY

We can trust him with our sexuality! He will elevate our longings for strength and beauty when our desires are too low. He will help us to rein in illusory and exaggerated desires. He is the epitome of strength and beauty—founded on him, yielded to his Spirit, we can aspire to both—to perceive and bless beauty and strength in others, and to receive that blessing in turn.

Just as submission to Christ is essential to navigating well these desires, so is his community. Trusted Christians are crucial in helping us to know the limits that liberate desire. Using the metaphor of the "gatekeeper" again, we can grow in godly discernment as we "submit to one another out of reverence for Christ" (Ephesians 5:21). With Christ and his community, we mature in moral decision-making, that is, the capacity to discern good and evil (Hebrews 5:14). He helps us. He knows we must choose daily what to let into the house and what to exclude. And sometimes others see what we cannot.

Energized by newfound feelings toward his new female friend, Rick rushed in with characteristic charm (and ignorance) and flung open the door of his heart to her. He did not realize that a relationship required more than the sensation of attraction. She was naive in her experience with men and quickly fell for him. His passion quickly flipped to disdain for her when she began to exhibit real need for him. He was not ready to bear the weight of that need; he wanted good feelings, not demands. The flame fizzled for him, and he slammed the door.

The effect was confusion. She felt hurt, even betrayed by his withdrawal. A wise man in his community corrected Rick: "Women are not your experiments in desire but image-bearers who need respect. For you, slow and steady is key. Let friendship—real engaging—temper your desire. Don't get ahead of yourself. Remember, another human being's heart is also at stake!"

Lucy was falling in love and hated it. She wanted to run from this man who drew near to her. She knew that if she opened the door of her heart to let him in, he would have power to reject her. She wrestled hard with her fears. And that fear threatened to capsize the good gift of an opposite-sex friendship! Grate-fully, she had two friends who helped her to see that she could grow in relationship with this man without giving everything away to him. She could open the door slowly and simply enjoy the exchange without making it the threatened end of her romantic life.

In talking it out with her community, Lucy discovered that she nourished extreme beliefs of this man's power—his power to make or break her life. Her friends reminded her that she was surrendered to Jesus—he was the One who deemed her valuable. She was more subject to divine beauty and strength than to those qualities in a mere man. That gave her authority. In Christ she had something valuable to give and to keep giv-ing—to this man and to those yet to come.

Lucy and Rick discovered something important in their sexuality: the power of community to help them grow. Given their surrender to Christ and to his Body, I could see signs of resurrection. Both were growing in love—learning in fits and starts how to open themselves up to another. And neither backed down from the hard truth that such an endeavor exposes weakness as much as it does the prospect of strength and beauty.

SPOTTING SELF-DECEPTION

The cycle of surrender continues: more exposure, more opportunity to know Jesus and oneself; all toward the end of becoming a better gift to others. Sobered by weakness, we may just be in a better place to respond to Christ's call to love well. Being raised with Christ first demands the humiliation of self-discovery. "Discernment requires, from the onset, one's consistent tendency toward self-deception."

A personal example may punctuate this point. A few years ago, I was mentoring a new leader and became aware that I was going out of my way to spend time with him. He liked the attention, and I felt at first that our relationship was simply a good fit. When I began to experience sexual attraction for him, I dismissed it. "My feelings aren't that strong . . . I can handle this."

My wife noticed my "attentiveness" to this person; I was tempted to brush it off but thought again, *Maybe I am not seeing this clearly.* I have an accountability group with three friends with whom I share difficult things—nothing is out of bounds. And yet, I wanted badly for this friendship to be none of their business. They all knew the guy in question; it was humiliating to admit that I was still working out issues related to same-sex attraction, especially because none of the three had that background.

So I stammered out my uncertainty about this friendship. And they prayed. I did have to confess adultery of heart, and I needed cleansing and forgiveness for it. Public confession gave me an actual boundary. That clarified the truth that in Christ the friendship would remain merely that. Lines broken by fantasy became solid once more. That is the grace of God.

My friends also provided wisdom. "Keep imparting to him as a leader, but do so within reasonable limits—limits we will hold you to." Those boundaries included ministry opportunities with this man that involved other people and excluded an open-ended relationship as friends with him. Friendship seemed unwise at the time, due to his need to see me clearly as a mentor. I simply communicated to him my desire to focus on ministry matters and not to muddle things with friendship, which is inherently mutual. (That actually shifted a year or so later when I had worked through my feelings and was actually free to be his friend, a passage my accountability partners and my wife recognized.)

Had I not acknowledged my mixed motives in this relationship, I could have been confusing to this man. He needed me to love him well by upholding boundaries that kept our mentoring relationship clear. And those boundaries gave me room to work out my issues safely, with people who love me and keep me accountable.

The good news: we can make wise moral decisions that free us to love well. Everyone benefits from this—ourselves, our loved ones, those we serve, and the greater community around us. We love well when we choose well for love's sake, forsaking the impulse of the moment.

God alerts us through his Spirit and his community when we may be deceiving ourselves. I now welcome that feedback. I want to be alive and well to the "gatekeeping" that frees all involved to value each other authentically. That means delineating needy emotional and sensual motives from the free desire to bless and build up another. What we recognize, we can decide for or against. His Spirit and Body help us in our weakness to love well!

Here we must walk humbly before both God and our fellow humanity; few if any are altogether free from self-deceiving tendencies. Profound and often outside of our immediate grasp, these tendencies may tempt us to believe that we are motivated by godly love when we are actually motivated by our need. We then run the risk of using others to meet our needs rather than valuing them, the true and godly goal of our sexuality.

Seem impossible? Not with the indwelling Spirit and trustworthy friends. It's all about humility—when we are surrendered to Christ and established in a caring community, we welcome promptings as to when and how much to open the gate of our hearts. God ennobles us by the strength and beauty of others when we wisely aspire to bless what is strong and beautiful in them. That requires choice. And we can make solid moral decisions about our relationships when we know we are deeply loved and valued. And when we know that what is at stake is a "who"—another living, breathing temple that bears the mark of the Creator.

No matter how we feel, we recognize that God has given us the authority to either ennoble that one through our love, or devalue them through confusing, even defiling behavior.

Such moral decision-making can result in transcendent experiences of love and creativity. Regardless of the outcome of our friendships (especially with the opposite sex), each has the potential to fill our houses with glorious glimpses of strength and beauty.

Lucy began to experience the goodness of masculine love and attention from the man she befriended. She slowly opened her heart to him, as did he to her. She blessed him with her valuable feminine presence, now lit from within by her delight in this particular opposite-sex relationship. She felt alive; it was as if her world had gone from black and white to Technicolor. The value she felt from the Father was being confirmed and enhanced and fleshed out by a particular man who wanted her and whom she wanted as well. She was falling in love.

Sadly, it became clear that both were moving in different directions—Lucy with an eye on the poor in her city and he intent on pursuing a demanding career that would take him overseas. They agreed that marriage was not to be the result of their feelings of love for each other. Painful. He moved away soon after, and they agreed it best to not mess with each others' emotions by transitioning into being "buddies." Sometimes love is not all you need.

In facing that fact, Lucy faced the truth of exclusion. Not only could an honorable opposite-sex friendship include her, it could also end. But would this be a rejection, another in a long line of disappointments? In other words, would the absence of this man transport her back to Kansas after transcendent moments in Oz?

LOVE THAT REMAINS

Adult gatekeepers like Lucy, united with Christ, can make good choices. If the relationship is healthy, full of good affection without veering into sensual excess or emotional manipulation, then one can choose to retain the goodness of the friendship deep within. It becomes a blessed memory that can serve as a tribute to what man can be for woman, and vice versa. As with parents, the power of the past relationship becomes foundational. Its memory urges one to not hide one's heart but to remind one that the offering is worth giving. In the Lord, even disappointing conclusions to relationships can engender courage and value.

Lucy opted for that. She felt the loss of friendship. But unlike the dreadful "gray" of disqualification she had felt in the past, this was a clean, sharp pain of grief that ultimately resulted in peace. Sorrow evolved into a renewed vision for relationships to come. She simply knew more of who she was, and what she wanted to give and receive from men in the days to come. The end of one relationship actually prepared her to be a better gift in the future.

What are some of the hallmarks of solid decision-making in relationships? How can we choose well and thus grow from the strength and beauty of the other? Paul gives us some clues in Ephesians 5:8-21. I love the final verse of this passage: "Submit to one another out of reverence for Christ" (Ephesians 5:21). That passage is the Magna Carta of healthy dating relationships. Out of holy fear and honor of Christ, submitted to him as the Lord of the "temple," we can seek to honor others. As always, it is his Spirit and Body that enable us, in fits and starts, to realize that honor in opposite-sex friendship.

Paul begins by reminding the sexually broken Ephesians who they are. Relationally, they had troubled backgrounds, not unlike our own. As I mentioned earlier and will elaborate upon in the next chapter, their relational grid, like ours, would have been as pagan as it was Christian. When I say "pagan," I mean that historically the Ephesians would have used one another to satisfy their sexual desires. They would have been self-serving, frustrated, and yet still greedy—an example of our consumer-driven approach to sex and relationships today (Ephesians 4:19; 5:3-7).

Greed is an important root of our relational sin; it's the drive behind all lust. Insecure and insensitive to the effect of our poor choices, we grasp after what is not ours to have. Rick wanted an image of love, not the labor love requires, while Bev still longed for the arms of a woman to protect her, Jake wanted power over a woman, Carmen constructed a personal image of wholeness and control while Fernando sought images on a computer screen. Lucy was inclined toward masculine love without the threat of pain or risk. All stemmed from a kind of greed, a kind of lust—the desire to possess what was not theirs to have.

Not in Christ, anyway. In that tension between their Christian commitments and a kind of lust, all felt shame, the emotion of disqualification. Like a veil composed of failures and flaws, shame rolled in quickly, like a fast-moving cloud cover, tempting them to hide once more. Shame had power to become for each of them a kind of tomb. Shame hid the truth of the beauty and strength each brought into their relationships.

A LIGHT GREATER THAN SHAME

Paul challenges that shame. He would not allow the Ephesians to hide the truth that Jesus had actually raised them up from the dead of sin and shame. Paul reminds them who they are. He declares: "For you were once darkness, but now you are light in the Lord" (Ephesians 5:8). He is reminding them, You are new, Jesus is raised from the dead and raises you with him; God's glorious light has overcome the power of shame! "Arise, shine, for your light has come, and the glory of the LORD rises upon you!" (Isaiah 60:1).

Shame is so profound and familiar to most people that these words need to be spoken, even shouted over and over until one gets this central truth: "What Jesus has done for me on the cross is more powerful than the shame I feel." We must remember this truth and recall it as often as necessary. Until we really believe it. We need to fight for each other until objective truth becomes more binding in our lives than lies and deadening emotions.

The house defined by the cross is full of light, a light that reveals its inspired beauty and manifests power to pierce that veil of familiar shame. In that light, one can then humbly and steadily arise in the true self to love others with increasing clarity and confidence. That is the self capable of knowing and extending the good gifts she or he has to offer, in truth.

I remember a prayer time I had with some friends over the failure I felt as a husband and father. I had many reasons I could give, all born of weariness and a convergence of disappointments. Unclean thoughts and shame settled on me like flies on a wounded man. My friends just said: "Andy, you are a man made new." They reminded me of Lazarus whom Jesus raised from the dead. Their job was just to respond to Jesus' command to the disciples to "Take off his grave-clothes and let him go" (John 11:44). The Body of Christ, inspired by the Spirit, helped remove the layers of sin and shame. Underneath emerged a new man, raised with Christ, awaiting fresh opportunity to arise and shine in my true self.

Having been raised by Christ, alive to his glorious light, we then need to act like it in our relationships. So Paul exhorts us all: act according to who you are. He says: "Live as children of light (for the fruit of light consists in all goodness, righteousness and truth) and find out what pleases the Lord" (Ephesians 5:8-10). Jesus was calling the Ephesians to manifest the new light operating within them. Having fundamentally transformed them from self-seeking to God-inspired, he awakens their conscience in regards to how they are treating one another. He calls them to represent him in how they conduct themselves relationally and sexually.

At the core, that involves the freedom to bless and honor one another as children of light—to behold in each other the truth that this other is valuable. However dishonor may have sought to define him or her in the past, he or she is now a vessel of honor. Period. Treat him or her accordingly.

We need to rejoice in the good gift of being raised with Christ in this body; he has raised us up to bless other bodies and so enhance the other's inspired strength and beauty. That means the capacity to relish the desirability and value of the real people whom God has put in our lives. We then bless and build them up. In every interchange, we as children of light can rejoice: we are raised up by the glorious One to mirror to others their strength and beauty as children of light.

We need to major on the business of blessing and building up one another. I am convinced that this is the ground on which many of us will discover particular unions that become binding, even marital ones. But in this we must still be realistic about the power of familiar strains of greed and shame. We must be realistic about the grave clothes that remain on us, and our dark power to place those rags on others as well.

FRUITLESS DEEDS

Paul exhorts us to "have nothing to do with the fruitless deeds of darkness" (Ephesians 5:11). That "darkness" may apply to many ways in which we have been greedy and dishonoring of others, then ashamed and unable to be the good gifts we want to be. It may involve obvious sin patterns, like habitual use of Internet porn, or crossing sexual lines with a non-spouse. It may be fantasy and dreamy, unexpressed yearnings that crowd out real prospects of relationship. It may be much more subtle, like bitterness or envy or hatred toward others, even toward an entire gender. It may involve giving too much, submitting foolishly to one who has yet to earn the right of our self-offering. It may be withholding oneself on the pretense of being too spiritual; that may be a mere defense against the defects we perceive in ourselves, the threat of being rejected. "If others only knew the truth . . ."

Surely there are many "religious" reasons that we withhold ourselves from others. Though passive, these too constitute deeds of darkness toward children of light. Included in these deeds are the ways we generalize about the other gender and demean them in turn. We can refer to the "other" in stereotypes that reveal our contempt for men or women in general, for example, men as sex addicts/animals, cut off, disconnected, cruel, passive/ineffectual, destined to disappoint; women as emotional, overwhelming, needy, control freaks, etc. No one is justified in generalizing about one-half of the population based on one's own broken experience.

And the way we demean those with same-sex attraction! In spite of politically correct tendencies in Western culture, we still ridicule those who struggle with homosexuality. If we are truly to be the house of God, full of his light, then we must guard the dignity of those who struggle with homosexual desire by silencing those who demean them.

Perhaps Paul's main point in this passage is to highlight misuses of the body. Paul refers to those misuses as immorality, impurity and greed (Ephesians 5:3). Included here are ways we take shortcuts to intimacy. Impassioned by the other's strength or beauty, we are apt to act greedily and partake of what is not yet ours. We may do so on the pretense of giving the other pleasure. But doubtless we are more motivated by our own desires and ignorant of what we provoke in the other that constitutes a kind of darkness. That darkness Paul defines as "fruitless."

Jake knew well the misuse of sexuality. He used the power of physical touch and mild forms of stimulation to awaken women's desire for him, which then led to more obvious sexual violations, including oral sex and intercourse. He used his body and other bodies to gratify himself, provoking confusion, defilement and hostility.

BOUNDARIES THAT PROTECT AND HONOR

I am asked often by singles what the limits of physical expression in dating are. How far can a child of light go with another before the light goes out? My answer is a simple one: physical disclosure must align with one's commitment to another. In other words, keep your clothes on until you get married. Inspired sexual love is all about *creativity*—that is, fruitfulness that results from one man and one woman submitting themselves to one another for life. Joining physically confirms over and over again the essence of self-giving: yielding one's most intimate offering to another, while confirming the good gift that the other is. And all the while experiencing the pleasure of the other's offering!

It is a marvelous deal that God employs as the basis for new life. Children are the fruit of becoming one flesh. God indwells that union—he is honored in it as the two houses merge and learn to submit households, one to another. There one is free to be naked and without shame (Genesis 2:25). The newly joined houses are ready for new life.

Now obviously we cannot go from casual friendship to one-flesh union without deepening our "knowing" of another on less intensive levels. I see this as a gradual disclosure, an unveiling of who one is on spiritual, emotional and physical levels. As the relationship unfolds, so must our disclosure on all three levels.

It is fruitful to develop the trust required to pray honestly together and to disclose our fears; it is fruitful too to share our affection verbally, as well as with a kiss and a gentle stroking of the cheek. We are becoming known by this other in a way that is authentic and apt. That is the fruitful and progressive unveiling that helps us to make an ultimate decision—will this be my life partner? If not, then good boundaries help us to sort through the loss of romance without the inflammation caused by having exposed too much to a "friend."

What then are "fruitless deeds"? These are disintegrated acts in which we provoke one another to sexual arousal without first attending to the emotional and spiritual maturity of the relationship. We need to first become known with our clothes on.

It is all too easy to lead out with acts that deliberately arouse the other: intensive kissing, holding and touching. Sexual arousal, if provoked prematurely, naturally leads to orgasm. And orgasm is the means by which we create new life—children. Aren't we then in error to deliberately provoke another to release and/or receive the man's seed before the two are prepared to welcome the fruit of such a passionate exchange?

God is just; he wills that we mature into emotional and spiritual partnership with another. That alone prepares us to raise the children we create. So the unmarried sin when they provoke another's sexuality prematurely. We simply have not earned the right to do so. Arousal can be contained when it is slowly integrated into disclosure at other levels, like the emotional and spiritual. We can get to know another without seeing his or her nakedness; we can express our desire without provoking orgasm. We commit fruitless deeds when we cross those two lines as unmarried people.

Nakedness without shame and orgasm without guilt are ours only upon making a lifetime commitment to this other. Before that, one is not ready "to know" the other's body. We are not prepared for it; we are not ready for a baby. So if we expose our nakedness to another before marriage, we should feel both shame and guilt. We failed to do the hard work necessary at

both emotional and spiritual levels. We have committed fruitless deeds of darkness.

Let me define my terms. Keep your clothes on. Make your
delights and fears and weaknesses and triumphs known. Confess sin and praise God together. Let words disclose more than
your sensual body language. Let your body convey the truth
that you are moving slowly because you do not yet actually
know the other well enough to yield your body to him or her.

Intimacy with another is about communication—making
oneself known to this other verbally. And physically, it means
growing in the capacity to reveal oneself on non-orgasmic levels.
In that process, we will feel much desire for this other. But we
learn to express it with words, acts of kindness and tender physical gestures, not by aiming for an orgasm. That includes appropriate displays of affection—good touch that confirms the desirability of the other without provoking the other to orgasm.

Sexual orgasm with another unites us with someone for life.
The power of that bond gets encoded on our memory long after
the relationship ends. It clutters our image of that one for the
rest of our lives. The old lover has power to harass us in our
marriages. Premature sexual arousal and orgasm are fruitless
deeds. God forgave me for my years of porn use and immoral
relationships. But he did not entirely free me from sin's consequence—a memory full of sensational, delusional images that I
can summon from my "bank" to this day.

I realize how conservative and nearly impossible this ethic
may appear. But perhaps we perceive it as products of a greedy,
consumer-driven culture that demands "I must have what I
feel." We have been provoked by images of sensational desire
all our lives; we can barely imagine what it may mean in a real
relationship to wait, to deny ourselves for another. But that's
just the point: we are dealing with a real person, a child of light

and honor, not one destined to gratify us for however long we are amused or stimulated. This is a person—a representative of the living God. We should tremble at the prospect of defiling him or her.

God wants our relationships to be essentially creative. Raised with him, full of light and life, we can learn to open ourselves appropriately to the wholesome gift before us. We can rejoice that we are growing in our capacity to give and receive love in ways appropriate to the maturity of the relationship. In so doing, we confirm that we are children of light.

Children of light detect fruitless deeds of darkness. In adherence to Paul's command, we can expose them when they threaten the relationship. We refuse them and thus forsake the shame and guilt they engender. God gives us authority to be free from fruitless deeds, and free for this lovely other. The result? Fruit that remains in our relationships, whether they become marital ones or remain friendships.

PEOPLE OF THE LIGHT TELL THE TRUTH

We are created for fruitfulness in our relationships, and yet we are still prone to fruitless deeds. (Paul was writing this to Christians, after all!) Here we see how the light cuts both ways. On the one hand, Jesus the Light has unique authority to shine on us and to reveal what is best and highest and true about our real selves—real because we are raised with him, his light reflecting that goodness. On the other hand, the light of Christ reveals what is still dark in us. "Everything exposed by the light becomes visible, for it is light that makes everything visible. That is why it is said: 'Wake up, O sleeper, rise from the dead, and Christ will shine on you'" (Ephesians 5:13-14).

Perhaps that is an aspect of the real self in relationships: we who are raised with him have a unique authority to see what is true in us and in our relationships. At the same time, light frees to name boldly what is false. Having been exposed, we then have power to expose ourselves. Put another way, light secures our value, helps us to see it; light also exposes the way we still devalue others or allow ourselves to be devalued. If Jesus does that, then we must cooperate with him and say what we see.

That is where his Spirit and Body are crucial. Both inform the "gatekeeper" (which is ourselves) and help us to make the kind of decisions that bear fruit. Bev found a support group in her church with whom she could walk out of a series of unhealthy, overly dependent relationships with women. She felt lonely and exposed, but her friends helped her. None of them came out of a background of same-sex attraction, yet they understood loneliness and could see the awesome woman Bev was. They blessed that truth and welcomed her to rely upon them, within limits.

For Bev, female friendships had been all or nothing—either consuming or absent. So to learn that other women could be warm and consistent yet non-exclusive was a revelation. She also began to see the way she manipulated others to draw them into a kind of maternal, "care-for-me" way. Or else.

One friend in particular helped her to see that she was not on the edge of peril, that she could sustain her life without the constant attention of one particular woman. In the meantime, these friends loved her as well as they could in light of their busy lives. Bev discovered she could give and receive love in a new way—a way the Lord had made for her. She felt valued; at the same time, she felt sobered by the broken patterns she was learning to see and say and overcome.

LIGHT BRINGS UNDERSTANDING

"Be very careful, then, how you live—not as unwise but as wise, making the most of every opportunity, because the days are evil. Therefore do not be foolish, but understand what the Lord's will is" (Ephesians 5:15-17). Honoring one another in one's body and in the one Body of Christ—that is God's will for adults seeking to glorify him in how they love.

Rick was learning the truth the good hard way. One key he learned was to slow down and just be friends with women. He also learned that it was important to make his intentions known if he were intent on pursuing a more exclusive friendship. He gave confusing signals to the first woman—turning on the charm, becoming too tactile, when he was just excited to feel sparks!

He was learning to steward desire quietly, thinking first of the other before himself. And he learned that such truth-telling cut both ways. In the course of a deepening friendship with yet another woman (this man was eager!), she made it clear to him that she was not interested in a more serious relationship with him. That hurt Rick, but helped him to grasp the truth that love can include as readily as it excludes.

If one walks in the light, aware of another's beauty and strength, they can still enjoy that beauty even if one sets a boundary. Here one needs to be reminded of one's intrinsic value, a value that need not be diminished for long by the decision of another created being.

The sting of rejection, the joy of being wanted: no way to avoid either if one is truthful about the "you-me" dimension of romantic love. Can honor still prevail when one faces the peril of not being wanted by one much desired? Yes. But not without continually reminding oneself that the goal is Christ—not romance, marriage or sex, but Jesus manifested in how we treat one another, in how we convey value to the other even and especially if the relationship fails to spark. Nowhere does that need to be more carefully lived out than in the pursuit of intimate, you-me relationships. That's why the Bible includes so much about it. That's why we need to carefully consider how we convey our desires to draw near to another. That applies pointedly to those who have damaged others.

Jake was on a short leash to just learn to be friends with women. It was excellent. He had to learn how to live a sober life, free from his tendency to seduce women. He took seriously Paul's words; they conveyed well his good hard task in the days ahead: "Do not get drunk with wine, which leads to debauchery. Instead, be filled with the Spirit. Speak to one another in psalms, hymns and spiritual songs. Sing and make music in your heart to the Lord, always giving thanks to God the Father for everything, in the name of our Lord Jesus Christ" (Ephesians 5:18-20).

He faced the good hard task of opening up his mouth alone to bless and build up women as friends. Like many others, alcohol often played a major role in his former exploits. A support group of recovering addicts helped him maintain a double sobriety: from drugs and the drug of sensuality that had so marred many lives. He was learning to become a serious gatekeeper.

Context mattered. Staying in a Spirit-filled context where Jesus was lifted up and where the goal was merely him and confirming others in him: that was the task he needed to learn before moving on to other more exclusive types of relating with women. Jake was learning to be faithful. The body around him was faithful. God through his Spirit was faithful to begin to restore his body as one of honor, not dishonor, so that he might honor others.

Friendship in which we, raised with Christ, delight in the strength and beauty of the other, is the base. On that base, much good can come: we have rich opportunity to know who we are as children of light who can deal with the shadows that remain. Passing through those shadows, we enter the dance of beauty and strength that is an exquisite and inspired gift from God to his created ones. The Lord of the house makes the difference. He fills us, and surrounds us by his Body. That liberates our good gatekeeping, or decision making. We thrive in this body. We fulfill Paul's exhortation "to submit to one another out of reverence for Christ" (Ephesians 5:21).

In both strength and beauty, we manifest God's very essence as we learn to love one another well.

6

CLEANING HOUSE

INTIMACY AND AUTHORITY

Has this house, which bears my Name, become a den of

robbers to you?

JEREMIAH 7:11

Heaven is my throne,

and the earth is my footstool.

Where is the house you will build for me?

Where will my resting place be?

ISAIAH 66:1

In order to love well, we must rid ourselves of idols. Sensual gods and goddesses readily enslave us; they weaken both our devotion to God and our freedom to love others. When we worship idols, three things may occur. We break the boundaries of commitment; we scramble the complementarity between men and women; and we focus on self, not God or others. You could say that idolatry ultimately results in the worship of the self. Gratefully, God gives us authority to name and destroy our idols so that love can be restored. We make war on idols in order to make holy love. We clean house so we can genuinely welcome others.

My teenage son came home one night, bypassed us quickly in his bulky sweatshirt (strange for a hot summer night . . .) then raced upstairs. Having been a sneaky teen myself once, I knew the signs. I bounded after him to find him in the act of stashing a bunch of porn DVDs under his bed. Busted. And wide open for redemption. I could hardly be angry at him. I remembered in a flash my mom finding porn in my room as a teen, and her saying slowly as she leafed through the magazine: "Each one of these people is a son or daughter, has a mother and father . . . these are real people."

True. Sexual images distort reality; they invite us to reduce people to their parts. And sexy idols rob us of our capacity to relate to real people. I felt all of this like a flood for my poor son, caught like a deer in the headlights. And I knew what we had to do. We had to destroy the idols before they could do anymore damage to my son's house. We both realized that urgent action was needed; we made a pact the next morning to obliterate them with baseball bats and gasoline. (He liked anything flammable.) Before he slept I told him a bit of my own story and God's grace to set me free from the idolatry of porn use and how he freed me to love real people, one woman in particular. ("Yeah, we've met," he said sarcastically.)

The next day we toppled the altars represented by those DVDs. As they blazed on the patio of our backyard, we agreed that fighting against idols is really about fighting for relationship with real people.

It is part of the hard good work of preparing for a real person, and about respecting the "other" enough to not reduce him/her to genital parts. It's about exercising our authority as Christians to get free and stay free from idols. It is about the first commandment: "I am the LORD your God, who brought you out of Egypt, out of the land of slavery. You shall have no other gods before me" (Exodus 20:1-3).

HOLY INTOLERANCE

One of my favorite passages involves Jesus cleansing the temple (John 2:13-17). Here "the lamb that was slain" is at his least tolerant and inclusive. Here his radical love rids God's house of all within that does not manifest him. Jesus does not dialogue with these detractors—he whips both man and beast and drives them out, overturning tables and shouting: "Get out!" He is consumed with zeal for God's house (John 2:17), less concerned about seekers than about the fractured face of his Father that seekers will find there if these temple robbers are allowed to remain. He cares about what goes on in the temple because the temple represents God to others. It is, after all, the house of the Creator.

The temple robbers were idolaters. They wanted to distract the people with seemingly "religious" practices that satisfied the robbers' greed and lust, as well as the religious "impulses" of the seekers. Neither pleased God. Neither led to real worship; in fact it dulled real devotion. So much so that Jesus excluded them forcibly from the house of his Father.

I am God's house. I am capable of entertaining within my walls robbers that tempt me to return to idolatry, to my old Egyptian practices. Each of us is like a cathedral, with many side chapels leading to the main altar. Over that altar is a huge crucifix. Many worshipers in the cathedral rarely reach the main altar—we are enchanted by the peculiar offerings in the side chapels. We give fleeting attention to Christ.

My "cathedral" is still vulnerable to housing sensual idols: sexy gods and goddesses that have power to defile the temple and cripple my capacity to love others well, especially my wife. I take account as I position my house before Jesus: what has entered my temple that defiles me, tempts me to break my vows and blocks my vision of him? He is faithful to bring up those faces that have triggered my familiar idolatry. I release them quickly to God, doing my part to cast out of the temple images that provoke false desire. Like Christ, I do not dialogue with them—I expel them.

United with Christ, my heart is softened by fresh mercy. And my will is alert and intolerant to enemy invaders. In that way, Jesus frees me yet again to offer myself to others, especially my wife, in a manner that she deserves and that I promised. Like the psalmist, I shall seek to "walk in my house with blameless heart. I will set before my eyes no vile thing" (Psalm 101:2-3).

True intimacy with Jesus inspires authority to clean house. The effect of a clean house? We can deepen intimacy with him and with those we long to love most. That requires daily decision-making. I can then line up with Joshua: "Now fear the LORD and serve him with all faithfulness. Throw away the gods your forefathers worshiped beyond the River and in Egypt, and serve the LORD. But if serving the LORD seems undesirable to you, then choose for yourselves this day who you will serve. . . . But as for me and my household, we will serve the LORD" (Joshua 24:14-15).

The clarity of my house begins with me; these are the daily vows I make to stay true to Jesus in my interior life. These vows involve boundaries—acting in love and in the limits appropriate to the relationship. And they involve staying true to the call to bless and honor the opposite gender and particularly my wife. Any choice to live outside of that complementarity and commitment constitutes a kind of idolatry. It involves me raising myself above the Creator and declaring: "I will worship any image that pleases me!" In essence, I am saying: I will worship myself and its desires.

I am still making daily decisions for freedom from idolatry. While researching this chapter, I read an article on how Internet porn was making the traditional porn industry obsolete. It cited a particular porn site that offered free everything: any image, any age, any configuration of man or beast. Having been raised on the traditional variety of porn (I was a good ol' traditional idolater), I could not imagine that. But the rat in me wanted to. I briefly scanned that website and was nearly overpowered by all the options. And shocked: how accessible, free and easy it has become to worship the creature and blacken the eye of its Creator.

Knowing my tendency for that idolatry, and how precious and hard won the freedom is that I know now, I realized how quickly I could be consumed by it once more. I stormed the bedroom where Annette was and promptly confessed to her what happened before anything else could transpire. (I then secured Covenant Eyes, a program through which another person has access all the time to what one is doing on the Internet, thus holding the weak ones like me accountable. See <www.covenanteyes.com>.)

To better understand those who battle persistently with familiar idolatry like Internet porn, it may be helpful to grasp my early religious history. Though I was raised Episcopalian, I actually devoted myself to sensual gods and goddesses. It was nothing short of a religion, its roots deep in pagan history where sex became the means of worshiping fertility gods.

In these early cults, sensuality was mistaken for heavenly

power and pleasure. I felt the same: in my awkward gender in-security, pornography empowered me. It led first to worshiping mere images of people, then evolved to devoting myself to real people through habitual sexual sin. In this, I violated God's call upon his human image to complementarity and commitment. False worship led to bondage to my own lusts.

The Bible references such idolatry as "revelry," the frenzied sensuality of the idolaters who surrounded the church or the nation of Israel and tempted her to prostitute herself. For ex-ample, the holy nation indulged in sexual immorality when she worshiped the Moabites' god, the Baal of Peor. Through sex, the pagans worshiped Baal; for Israel to join them meant that she prostituted herself, both sexually and in her divided spiritual loyalties. God's judgment of Israel was harsh. Twenty-three thousand died as a result of her idolatry (Numbers 25).

I was tempted to write the Old Testament references off. Then I discovered that Paul used these references to warn the believers at Corinth that they could face a similar judgment if they continued in their "pagan revelry" (1 Corinthians 10:6-13). In other words, the Corinthians' sexual immorality was a form of idolatry that warranted God's judgment.

Like Israel and the church at Corinth, I felt the sting of judg-ment in my body. Going outside the lines of complementarity and commitment in multiple homosexual unions, I began to experience all manner of communicable disease. Friends began to mysteriously die off; their bodies' natural defenses broke down in morbid agreement with the boundaries they were breaking. (Obviously, I "came out" before AIDS had a name.) My soul felt empty and yet needed more and more flesh in order to feel temporarily satisfied. At some intuitive level, I knew that I was bound. And getting scared. It seems that the sensual gods wanted blood.

Friends and family prayed for me. God was kind. And persuasive. It was as if God was imploring me as Paul implored the Corinthians: "The sacrifices of pagans are offered to demons, not to God, and I do not want you to be participants with demons" (1 Corinthians 10:20). These demons involved dark powers committed to binding me to an image far less than what Christ intended for me.

These familiar spirits had power—a power I gave them when I first exposed myself to pornography. I noticed early on that I had a strange authority to know where and when porn was available: in someone's home, or on TV. I would at once desire and discern it. It was as if I had invited a demonic presence that aided me in my pre-teen and teen addiction to porn. I had called out to another source for help in foraging for my idols. And help came in the form of an unclean, demonic presence. It guided and empowered my porn addiction. And then it advocated for me as I began to make idols of other people. There was often a real "presence" that guided my securing male partners.

In truth, idolatry is diabolical and gives demons access to our homes, our temples, our bodies, our churches. John Wimber asked me once why he felt unusual sexual temptation in a particular denomination where he often ministered. The answer was clear: the sexually permissive history of that denomination had morphed into blessing homosexual unions and ordaining gay clergy. It was no longer a safe house. Idolatry in policy and practice impacts us all. "You and I are more subject to familiar spirits in this denomination because they have permission to be here," I responded.

We begin with our own temples. My idolatry revealed its dead-end worship early on. I concluded that mere creatures could not complete me. I cried out for mercy. Into the broken ground of my body, Jesus descended and made his home. The reign of his kingdom brought a peace that composed me, in contrast to the agitated frenzy that marked my idolatry.

I still struggled a great deal with unclean thoughts, although I had made a decision to close the door on homosexual relationships. Seeking more help, I attended a weeklong seminar in which the speaker, Leanne Payne, called all who were internally struggling to come forward and make a decision. As I knelt at the altar, I felt tightness around my head and could see a swirl of pornographic images. The one praying for me instructed me to pick up the sword of the Spirit and destroy the sensual idols I had worshiped. I did so quietly, but decisively. I could see myself hacking up reams of pornographic materials then offering myself to Jesus afresh. He loosed a flood of blood and water that rose swiftly and removed the broken "idols" from my house.

I felt an immediate release from the pervasive pornographic thoughts to which I had grown accustomed. And I felt empowered to continue to guard my house from them. These temptations were familiar. The demons associated with these idols had had regular access to my house; I was just starting to contend against them! I felt clear and empowered to do so, yet a huge battle awaited me. Perhaps this is the major error of "deliverance" approaches to profound sexual habits. We do not adequately equip "the delivered" to do the battle necessary to refuse the familiar lures. So we cleanse the house for them, and leave them without recourse when the vultures return en masse.

My fight had just begun. I declared that night: "My house will not be a temple for robbers, those tendering the false gods and the sacrifices they demand!" I could see what was going on in the Spirit and I had strength to choose because I had aligned myself with Jesus Christ. Yet I knew that I must stay on the alert to enemy intrusion. I was beginning to have zeal for the holiness of my house.

FALSE LOVERS

Bev was far more fragile than I. She needed to be handled carefully in light of her abuse, the crack in her foundation on which her same-sex dependencies arose. Yet these dependencies constituted an idolatry that required her surrender and renunciation. Her body had been awakened to the power of feminine touch. She had habituated to these lovers who truly had become goddesses for her, a sensual refuge from her pain and loneliness.

She had begun to operate in the realm of familiar spirits—she could go into a room and spot out the vulnerable one and begin to move in on her. The enemy of her soul was committed to engaging her and others in the seductive dance at hand. She was greatly helped by strong and safe women in the Body of Christ who satisfied (within limits) her need for feminine friendship, but she also had to name and refuse the dark powers that had unwittingly engaged her in lesbian longing and activity.

During one healing session, Bev renounced her idols and the familiar spirits accompanying them. In particular, she broke ties that had bound her body to sensual memories of several women. She had thought all was well because the unions were long ended. But actually she drew upon their memory frequently as a refuge, often paired with masturbation, or at least the soulful longing for the "good old days." She needed to let go of the illicit "bonds," renounce them in Jesus' name, and rid herself of their reminders.

With God's help, Bev established a new boundary. After the renouncing and cleansing time, she realized that Jesus himself could become a wall of protection for her. She could call upon him at anytime, and he would be her fortress against the forces that would otherwise gladly lead her into temptation. Bev was beginning to realize the battle she was in. Her adversary wanted to destroy her; God wanted her to know her authority to seek refuge in him. He would be her boundary, a high tower against the enemy of her soul. He wanted to be more familiar to her than the demons!

She is still in training, and God is faithful to both protect her and to empower her to make the good choices she must to remain in protection of those good boundaries. He is the wall of fire around her; he is becoming her glory within (Zechariah 2:5). And she, like any former idolater, has a responsibility to keep her house free for God and the good gifts he gives though trustworthy members of his Body.

THE DARKNESS OF IDOLATRY TODAY

I believe that we are living in a time of unprecedented sexual and relational idolatry. The moral ozone layer has burned off. We are unprotected, burned daily by the breakdown of commitment and complementarity, and the rise of self-worship, that characterizes our age.

We used to flinch. In one five-minute segment on network TV the other day, I watched a commercial on men and women commenting graphically (and goofily) on penis size and the enhancement "drug" the men were taking (to which the women purred), an ad for a female exercise video in which housewives simulated strippers in order to get into shape, and a movie ad depicting a child with a bird-like demon manifesting grotesquely out of his mouth.

Such rot would have been forbidden five years ago. We stopped flinching. Idols sear our skin and we no longer feel it. Desensitized by all manner of evil, we gaze dully at yet another round of idolatry with bloodshot eyes. What we are witnessing is nothing less than a relational meltdown. Idols empower all the wrong things; they awaken lust and deaden conscience. We then act badly, in ways that rob us of clarity and virtue and leave us unfit for real relationships.

Maybe technological advances have something to do with it. We have access to multiple screens and their images, depicting scenarios that are wholly unfit for visual consumption; we are connected to everyone and yet not anyone, spending time fashioning an image of ourselves that hundreds may access without accessing anything that even approximates the intimacy we need.

The violence of porn. Let's describe the mangling of commitment inherent in porn use. Sex is intended to be experienced only between a man and woman who know each other painfully well and who have made a lifetime commitment to each other.

What then does it do to the soul that has been exposed thousands of times to images of others having sex? Porn strips sex of its only meaningful context. It fires up the libido but diminishes one's moral and emotional capacity to be a good gift to another. Thus viewing sex ultimately cripples one's capacity to have inspired sex.

And porn is as potent a temptation for believers as nonbelievers. A pastor of a booming church said to me that 80 percent of his male congregants under thirty years had a history with habitual porn use. "It would be different," he said, "if they were struggling against it. To many it's just not a big deal." A generation has been weaned on obscene virtual realities. One of the first e-mail messages my son received from a new friend in junior high was a list of really hot porn sites. That has now evolved into "sexting" in which kids offer themselves to each other via naked photos taken on cell phones. Then sent to whomever.

A generation is without a boundary. Repeated exposure to sex without commitment strips all involved of good shame and dignity and wisdom. All three are needed to form intimate relationships, which are about revealing oneself slowly and trustfully, one layer at a time. Now clothing has become optional. The porn-minded impose their bloodshot vision upon all living.

Porn is an expression of idolatry that distorts normal and good desire into perverse fire. That fire singes one's capacity to become a good gift to another—to cherish and value another, and be valued. And it's everywhere, unrestrained.

The Justice Department of the United States recently said: "Never before has so much obscenity been available in so many homes to so many minors with so few restrictions." One study on the effect of porn and the media concluded: "Constant exposure to beautiful women has made single men less interested in dating and married men less interested in their wives." In short, men are much less interested in the women available to them.

Raunchy soundtracks don't help. One young woman, a Christian, admitted that certain soundtracks were so paired with her history of sexual immorality that she could not listen to them. Makes sense. Men and women sound like equal opportunity idolaters in much of popular music. Music has power to become the listener's own soundtrack. We get fired up by some hipster's rendering of their own raunchy reality, lose our inhibitions and are inclined to make their story our own.

Promiscuity. You see it and hear it; then you do it. Your average college student has ten partners during his or her four years. The first national study on sex and female teens came out and revealed that one in four was infected with a sexually transmitted disease. Laura Vanderkan writes, "Hook-ups do satisfy biology, but the emotional detachment does not satisfy the soul.

That's the real problem—not the promiscuity but the lack of meaning."

Sex now seems like the new drug, a pleasing practice to be shared by friends. Neither commitment nor particular romantic intention seem to be required anymore, just attraction. I recall a shift in the nineties: some sitcom episodes started to feature sex between friends, shows like *Seinfeld*, then *Friends*. Yet in classic sitcom style, there was no negative consequence for getting naked with one's "friend." No ground was lost, just zany plot twists in which one morphed from friend to lover then back again. Comically. In twenty-two minutes. We took our cues.

We bought the lie that casual sex is free. In truth, it is costly. I remember the seismic shift that occurred in my first male friendship that became sexual. Friends lose friends when they become lovers. There is forgiveness but no return to original innocence. Jake learned this the hard way. His ex-girlfriends could forgive but not forgo the consequences of "friendly sex." Especially walking partners in the faith. J. Budziszewski writes: "Although sex consummates the friendship of husband and wife, it perverts the friendship of comrades."

Divorce. What happened? How has sex (real or viewed) without commitment flourished so? A contributing factor may well be divorce. A *Newsweek* cover story claims that in postwar culture, marriage was still the most powerful social force. Today divorce is. Today's young adults are the first generation to grow up in a culture where divorce superseded marriage. They learn fast: "The people I need and love most make promises with their bodies that they do not keep."

Carmen knew this well. Her father had left early on for another woman, devastating her mother. She grew up on the faultline of their fractured relationship, never sure if or when her father would come around and less sure of her mother's stability when he would. She feared Fernando's unfaithfulness, and she secretly resented people who struggled with sexual idols. In truth they threatened her well-being. After all, her father's sexy idol in the form of another woman did permanent damage to the family he sired then abandoned. Carmen at once hated divorce and feared its reoccurrence in her own marriage.

The occasional death of a marriage due to abuse or adultery or abandonment has become a way of life. Quality of life now trumps commitment. Is it any wonder that parents have little relational authority to impart to their kids? I contend that our divorce culture is the single biggest factor that underlies our culture of idolatry—sex without cost, love without perseverance. Today's credo: if your marriage does not work, move on.

Homosexuality. On that basis, the idolatry of forsaking complementarity arises. The reasoning is kind of simple: if commitment no longer counts in sexual relationships, why should gender? In the early nineties, Thomas Schmidt prophesied that homosexuality stood in the frontlines of all the forces seeking to shape the twenty-first century. His words have come true. In politics and academics, in the church, in the popular media and mindset, we are a people unsure as to whether man for woman and woman for man really matters in sexual unions.

Same-sex identity and relationships are now mainline. Kids leave home as Catholics and Nazarenes only to return home from university as bona-fide citizens of a gay nation. Disoriented parents scramble to make sense of it, usually siding with their kids' new "confirmation" as a way of managing a nearly overwhelming conflict.

Bev had no problem securing lesbian relationships at university, while Rick discovered a strange blend of spirituality and homosexuality in a Christian "mentor" in his community. His "friend" claimed that the Bible really did not have anything definitive to say about homosexuality and urged him to embrace the "gift" of his gayness by having sex with him.

Those struggling with same-sex desire face few restraints to act out those desires. Out of the closet and into our daily lives: homosexuality emerges as hip and shame-free, a sexy alternative to traditional idolatry. Especially in the popular media.

Oprah features "Lesbians at 30," a trio of glamorous women who left their husbands for each other, empowered by O's "live your truth" credo and a daffy therapist. In 2009, HBO represented gay and bisexual characters in 42 percent of its programming hours, *slightly* more than one might find in real life. Researchers cite the new freedom young men and women have to experiment with homosexually; what used to be shameful has evolved into something hip. Girls weary of guys turn to other girls; guys tired of "straight" idolatry peruse the Web for new thrills involving other guys. A generation champions freedom from gender constraints.

Yet the face of homosexuality fluctuates—on one hand, many argue for an inborn biological destiny, on the other, an evolving freedom to love the one you are with, regardless of his or her gender. Is freedom for homosexuality a birthright or another shrill demand for personal pleasure? "I feel, therefore I am"; "I want, therefore I must have." Has the relentless push for gay rights become an arm of our consumer culture? Have our drives, unevaluated, become the basis for determining what is just and true for the individual and those who surround him or her?

Gay activists strive relentlessly for the gold ring: full rights and privileges on par with heterosexuals. That involves full marriage and family rights, including "gay marriage." Now on some altars bride 1 and bride 2 aspire to be the image of God, invoking the holy in an earnest attempt to show all, "Yes, we really are normal."

I contend that neither marriages nor talk shows nor gay student unions can resolve the inner conflict in those who aspire to same-sex unions. Why? Because they unwittingly resist the Designer and Redeemer of all the living. In bowing down before the same gender, they seek in vain to be whole in an image that cannot complete them. Not really.

The problem with homosexual activity is that we strive for wholeness in a mirror image of ourselves. It is inherently narcissistic. Like the myth of Narcissus, a beautiful young man becomes mesmerized by his own reflection, and is condemned to the futility of becoming one with himself. Homosexuality is union with the same, not the other. It can never achieve the whole union that can only occur between two disparate parts: male and female.

In spite of its landmines, heterosexuality is the ground on which God calls us to work out our salvation, sexually speaking. Homosexuality thus constitutes a kind of idolatry—a raising of oneself and one's own desires above the Creator.

NARCISSISM: THE WORSHIP OF THE SELF

Rick knew his problem lay deeper than homosexuality: his greater barrier to love was a reluctance to offer himself wholly to another, regardless of gender. Like many, he loved the idea of relationship but had never exercised genuine self-giving. So he settled for presenting a charming and seductive image that another might adore but that would keep him separate, protected from any real risk or hard effort. He wanted to be worshiped.

Truly the idolatry of homosexuality, of forsaking complementarity, can and must be understood on this greater altar of the idolatry of self—the consummate narcissism that is the driving force behind all sexual and relational brokenness. We all know what this is, to varying degrees. It's all about deep hurt and control. Jake wanted to be the tough guy in control of women; Carmen wanted to contain her fear by becoming invulnerable to Fernando. Lucy wanted to be a saint, impervious to a man's rejection. They wanted to be adored without risk.

Idolaters are more comfortable with the false self that seeks attention than with attending to others. Fear drives this self, as do broken homes, the swirl of flickering images that drive and delude us on the Internet, the virtual communities we invest in that fuel the presumption that we can have love without offering the whole self.

How so? I am convinced that those whose connection with others is primarily virtual may run the risk of creating a self without ever having to reveal their true selves to others. Maybe it starts in chat rooms, where one can craft an image. One might just alter the truth a bit to spice things up. (For many this is the beginning of a sexualized, romanticized self based wholly on one's virtual manipulations.) So too on Facebook. It needs to be said that Facebook is a great tool for connecting with people. In good hands, it liberates a casual give and take of info. But for those who tend toward addiction and struggle to find roots in an actual community, Facebook may well defeat the very purpose it seeks to achieve.

Facebook frees one to create a "cyber-self" of photos and sound bites that is available for many to see. The more friends the merrier. But friendship based on what? Like characters in the reality shows we grew up on, a generation now generates "selves" for all to see, virtual calculations that include confessions, philosophizing, one's risings and fallings. But those who bare their intimate life in cyber-space may actually be reducing their capacity to connect in real life.

The basis for becoming a mature image-bearer is the capacity to form friendships based on good, hard progressive disclosure. The preciousness of the offering is defined by the depth of disclosure. The more depth, the fewer involved, and the more protection and discretion required. That may result in the ultimate disclosure—becoming naked (both emotionally and physically) and consummating marital communion—for no one but the two of you to experience.

On the other hand, virtual communities can create false intimacy and blur the necessary boundaries that are required of real intimacy with others. It may also foster a self not wholly founded on reality. One Harvard grad said of his countless Facebook friends: "I can now maintain hundreds of friendships without having to make any effort whatsoever." I contend that real friendship cannot exist without mature, face-to-face self-giving.

So we have virtual help in the formation of today's idolater. Not surprisingly, a recent study just announced that narcissism (as a diagnosable personality disorder) has reached an all-time high among college students. Most students rated themselves superior to their peers. They are also more likely than students twenty-five years ago "to have short-lived relationships marked by infidelity, a lack of emotional warmth, game-playing, dishonesty, and violent behaviors."

The idolater's creed is just that: "I can live my life any way I want," which means relationally, "when I am not getting what I want, I bail." Or worse.

LOSS OF THE TRUE SELF

At the core of this modern sadness is the failure to know and to express one's true self: full of need and yet more than that, a self created by God to give good gifts to others. A wise woman writes: "Perhaps the most enduring failure of love today lies in not revealing one's true self. The temptation to seem better than one is—to not risk the rejection truth might bring—is a perpetual one. We need great faith in the reality of love to dare present ourselves in naked truth to those we love."

God seeks to reclaim that self: the house capable of opening its doors wisely and well, risking the offering of one's true self in order to bless and build up others. And yet we live in a culture that seeks to rob that self through idolatry. Like you, I am part of this culture. My house rests on those fault lines like everyone else's. The gods and goddesses of this world beckon to me. None of us are unaffected: for some it is deeply personal, for others it is interpersonal as we watch loved ones being destroyed at the altars of sexual and relational idolatry.

WHO SHALL WE SERVE?

Never before have we had to answer Joshua's call, to turn from idolatry and serve God, more decisively. Which god will define our households? Or in Elijah's words: "How long will you waver between two opinions? If the LORD is God, follow him; but if Baal is God, follow him" (1 Kings 18.21).

Israel's challenge described in the Old Testament is not unlike what we as the church face today—both in our personal temples and in our corporate gatherings. God chose Israel out of all the other nations on the earth to be holy, his treasured one, reserved for him and him alone, like a beautiful bride for her husband (Deuteronomy 7:6). God set this people apart for the high call of revealing his unfailing love for all the other nations on earth to see. They revealed his love in the way they lived, the integrity with which they kept their covenants with each other. Especially in the sexual realm; what the Israelites did with their bodies mattered to the Lord. Just as God called Israel to reserve faithful worship to himself alone, so he commanded the people to manifest faithfulness to one another in monogamy.

One nation under one God sealed in one-spirit union; one woman for one man sealed in one-flesh union. Marital faithfulness revealed God's faithful love to Israel. So the sexual integrity and purity of Israel mirrored her spiritual integrity and purity.

Sure enough, when Israel was faithful to her God, she lived within the boundaries of sexual purity. But when she strayed from him, she defiled herself through the sexual practices demanded by the gods of other nations, like the Moabites and Canaanites. Spiritual idolatry and sexual immorality are intrinsically linked. The prophets decried such a toxic mix by warning the Israelites, "Do not defile yourselves in any of these ways, because this is how the nations that I am going to drive out before you became defiled" (Leviticus 18:24).

But she did defile herself. God defined Israel as a wayward spouse for her spiritual and sexual adulteries. Israel would not forsake Yahweh altogether, but she would establish two sets of altars: "Even while . . . worshiping the LORD, they were serving their idols" (2 Kings 17:41). She tried in vain to maintain both relationships.

God through the prophets demanded a decision. "You shall not make for yourself an idol in the form of anything in heaven above or on the earth beneath or in the waters below. You shall not bow down to them or worship them; for I, the LORD your God, am a jealous God, punishing the children for the sin of the fathers to the third and fourth generation of those who hate me, but showing love to a thousand generations of those who love me and keep my commandments" (Exodus 20:4-6).

In light of these stakes, nothing less than clear and decisive action will do. "Break down their altars, smash their sacred stones and cut down their Asherah poles. Do not worship any other god, for the LORD whose name is Jealous, is a jealous God" (Exodus 34:13-14).

Israel, the church and the Christian individual can readily become a house divided; we are fully capable of worshiping the true God while bowing before idols too. God asked the saints at Corinth to make a decision to forsake their idols. He did so by appealing to true spiritual communion with himself.

These new converts had worshiped the goddess Aphrodite through temple prostitution most of their lives; Paul implores them to forsake such familiar religion in favor of the One who loves them most. "What agreement is there between the temple of God and idols? . . . 'Therefore come out from them and be separate, says the Lord. Touch no unclean thing and I will receive you. I will be a Father to you, and you will be my sons and daughters'" (2 Corinthians 6:16-18).

RETURN TO THE FATHER

The apostle draws the Corinthians (and us) with such kindness: he manifests beautifully the Father's fullness of tenderness and strength. That fullness demands a choice. Powerful love is persuasive; like a lifeline thrown to those drowning, his wooing love makes repentance possible.

Tenderness is matched by insistence. Nothing less than the image of God in humanity was at stake. The false gods rendered the saints compulsive and self-serving. Paul called them to manifest the gospel through relationships marked by commitment and complementarity.

God's kindness is both splendid and stern. As Moses implored the Israelites:

> Now what I am commanding you today is not too difficult for you or beyond your reach. . . . No, the word is very near you; it is in your mouth and in your heart so you may obey it. See, I have set before you today life and prosperity,

death and destruction. For I command you today to love the LORD your God, to walk in his ways. . . . But . . . if you are drawn away to bow down to other gods and worship them, I declare to you this day that you will certainly be destroyed. . . . Now choose life, so that you and your children may live, and that you may love the LORD your God, listen to his voice, and hold fast to him. For the LORD is your life. (Deuteronomy 30:11, 14-20)

This jealous love is a call to return to intimacy with the Father. The militant command to cast out all idols from the temple is also an invitation to return to the covering of peace, the protective presence of the Bridegroom who is lovesick for his beloved ones, his bride. Although battered in our infidelities, we have never ceased to be beautiful in his eyes. He woos us with kindness, a love as intimate as it is jealous for our return to him.

Hosea 2:14-20 describes the ache of the humble King for us, his objects of desire:

> Therefore I am now going to allure her;
>   I will lead her into the desert
>   and speak tenderly to her.
> There I will give her back her vineyards,
>   and will make the Valley of Achor a door of hope.
> There she will sing as in the days of her youth,
>   as in the day she came up out of Egypt.
> "In that day," declares the LORD,
>   "you will call me 'my husband';
>   you will no longer call me 'my master.'
> I will remove the names of the Baals from her lips;
>   no longer will their names be invoked. . . .
> I will betroth you to me forever;

> I will betroth you in righteousness and justice,
> in love and compassion.
> I will betroth you in faithfulness,
> and you will acknowledge the LORD."

Wooed by love, our action must be decisive. How far will you flee from your beloved idol? How long will you fight? Will you secure the computer safeguards you need to forsake your fix? If you leap over your own boundaries, will you forsake your computers, or at least ensure another is present with you when using it? In other words, demonstrate your commitment to purity through action, not merely though another confession.

Develop a daily accountability system for checking in with a trusted friend. Text a friend daily and give an answer: clean or unclean? Some of us need that kind of accountability and if we look, we can find another who does too.

Set limits on the amount of time you spend in virtual community, including Facebook. Use that time instead to talk and pray with real people, in the flesh. Fernando went on such a fast and discovered he had spent approximately two hours a night online, while failing to adequately connect with his wife, Carmen. Turning off his computer was key to strengthening his marriage. It also allowed him to find solitude once more in his off-work hours. There God was calling him into deeper intimacy. Virtual realities cluttered the way.

If you are crossing sexual boundaries in a relationship, ask yourself: "Can I actually handle this relationship? Am I able to set godly boundaries and stay within them? Have I employed the help of the Body to be faithful to God in the relationship?" Be willing to lose the relationship if you cannot be true to the Lord in it.

In letting go of her last lover, Bev recounted how "her absence made room for the Lord to re-establish himself as Lord in my life. I guess I wanted her to be God; I looked to her to save me from my loneliness. Releasing her gave God ground to meet both of us in new ways. It was also the hardest thing I have ever done," she said tearfully.

This is where we need the community more than ever. We cannot be an idol-free house without the help of the greater house of God. How persistently, ruthlessly honest will you be with your community about the battle at hand? That is crucial. Refusing false gods and goddesses requires walking partners who stand with us as we seek to worship the One and refuse all else. At least two others need to know what we are up against— those who can keep secrets and who know how to pray and support us over the long haul.

This applies to those who have generational histories of sexual immorality and idolatry. We identify abuse, adultery, sexual addiction and perversion, etc. and ask God to clarify how we had lived out that inheritance. We then break its power through repentance and renunciation.

Carmen prayed to break the powerful threat of adultery and divorce that had been hanging over her. She wanted freedom from its emotional weight. She renounced those "sins of the father" and did what God instructed Gideon to do: "Tear down your father's altar to Baal and cut down the Asherah pole beside it. Then build a proper kind of altar to the LORD your God" (Judges 6:25-26). She did this by naming any way that generational idolatry had been passed down to her. Then, she took authority over that negative inheritance and declared: "As for me and my house, we will serve the LORD" (Joshua 24:15).

Carmen took authority in light of her choice today to walk Jesus' way in her marriage. Something broke in her. She wept; she arose and discovered a new freedom to believe that she could choose rightly and not be subject to the past determining her present.

Something extraordinary happened to Bev here too. As the victim of an uncle's abuse, she represented one of many women in her family historically that had been sacrificed at the altar of another's perversion. That abuser had been a relative, and thus the sacrifice was covered over in secrets and lies, as other family members scrambled to hide the truth and so protect the "family honor." She renounced that perversion and declared: "It is no longer mine, I never wanted it, and by God's grace I ask you Jesus to bind it away from me." He did, and it began a process of healing whereby, in light of his love, she could refuse that inheritance of perversion. Jesus had laid claim to her, and in his strength, she broke the abuser's claim on her life.

Worship is central to this freedom. Out of gratitude to the One who shed blood for idolaters like us and who lives to love and empower us to refuse the bloodthirsty gods, we worship him. We give him the first fruit of our day, our affections, our money, our relationships, our thoughts, our motives, our needs, our aspirations. We give him highest place: we sing to him or meditate upon the Scriptures that describe him; we abide silently with Love himself; we become sensitized to his presence and grow in intimacy with him. We learn to linger with him and readily detect and refuse intruders. He becomes our delight. We want no other. Then we love others out of the love received, earnestly seeking to manifest him.

Declaring war on our idols clears the way for holy love.

"Now fear the LORD, and serve him with all faithfulness. Throw away the idol gods your forefathers worshiped beyond the river and in Egypt, and serve the LORD. But if serving the

LORD seems undesirable to you, then choose for yourselves whom you will serve. . . . But as for me and my house, we will serve the LORD" (Joshua 24:14-15).

7

WHOLE HOUSES

OFFERING THE REAL SELF

Everyone who hears these words of mine and puts them into practice is like a wise man who built his house upon the rock. The rain came, the streams rose, and the winds blew and beat against that house; yet it did not fall, because it had its foundation on the rock.

MATTHEW 7:24 26

A house divided against itself will fall.

LUKE 11:17

Christians in the twenty-first century face a hard challenge. While under the divine command to work out our salvation together as male and female, we are also realists. Before us and all around us we see the wreckage of those who have tried and failed. The common solution of divorce, those who remain bound to cruel yet usual sins, the resignation to homosexual destiny, unhappy unwanted singleness—we behold these sign-posts as much as we do those image-bearers who seem to flourish in their sexual and relational selves.

GETTING REAL

Have relationships always been this complicated? Have our virtual lovers—the multiple screens that mesmerize us daily—ruined us for real people? Is the enemy of our souls that much stronger today than yesterday? Or do we simply have greater freedom to talk about the trash under our skin and bed covers? Maybe all the above.

Noteworthy today is the value placed on telling the truth, on getting "real," no matter the cost. Our six friends were perhaps the first in their family lines to uphold that value. Prior to that, their families upheld a code of honor. The greatest sin was not abusing a niece, committing adultery, porn addiction or a homosexual union—the greatest sin was getting caught. And so bringing dishonor on the family.

In other words, one might tolerate the sin as long as it did not trumpet itself in the public square. A system of honor keeps secrets, and is based on a mutual, unspoken agreement. As long as the sinner is discreet, the system defends the sinner by looking the other way. All six, however, grew up in a new world. Today, the lines between public and private reality have broken down. We know now that looking away from dishonorable things does not change their dreadful impact. Abuse, adultery, divorce, alcoholism—each of our friends was painfully aware of at least one of the above. They bore its wound.

Beyond wounds, each faced certain weaknesses. As flawed human beings, they knew that their offering to anyone was not wholly "pure." It was not enough to blame one's personal sinfulness on the sins of others. One cannot excuse his or her own cruel treatment of others on the insight that "I was treated cruelly in my youth." Somehow, by grace, each knew that they had to take responsibility for the unique weakness they bore and brought into relationships.

Grace had made the difference for each—a grace greater than sin, wounds or weakness. Each had been called up and out from the cosmos of one's family and culture. Jesus, tender and strong, called each into a new kingdom. Raised with Christ out of the mere determinants of a fallen world, each began to discover a new base of relating one to another.

Like Lazarus, the authentic self knows that its new base of relating is wholly born of a greater power, the power that raised Jesus from the dead! Jesus himself has called us out of the tomb of the secular self—the self defined and determined by forces other than grace. In response to his tender yet insistent call: "Come out of the tomb!" we learn to live according to his voice and presence.

Lucy recognized this voice when she was tempted to return to the tomb. While out with a guy she really liked, she could tell that it was not going well. He seemed distracted and disinterested. She felt that dreadful cloud cover roll in—the temptation to agree with another's disfavor: "Yeah, you're right, I am not worthy of your time and attention . . ." Sure enough, he excused himself early from the restaurant, muttering some lame excuse. But this time, she straightened up and remembered the strong and tender One who gave her breath.

She made a quick call to a friend who knew her tendency toward rejection. Together, they refused to concede to the tomb. Disappointed, yes; devastated, no. She had a self that another could not diminish because that self was born of Christ and his favor. God was in the house! He now ruled and reigned with her—in her own skin. And that real God wanted to free her to know and live out what it meant to offer herself authentically to others.

You could say that the authentic self needs encouragement. Secure in Christ, growing with others, she or he needs to discover regularly the strength and beauty they actually possess. Wise brothers and sisters can see the unrecognized, latent attributes awaiting expression. Such building up of others according to their needs is crucial to the authentic self (Ephesians 4:29).

Each of us possesses unaffirmed aspects of our humanity that must be identified and integrated into the new self Jesus has raised from the dead. Leanne Payne writes about this new self beautifully:

> We must differentiate between the self that collaborates with the principle of evil and selfishness and the self that abides in Christ and collaborates with him. That is the true self. That is the justified new creation, the soul that is saved and lives eternally. The former self we deliberately and continuously die to; the other we joyfully and in great humility and thankfulness accept. . . . It is only with the full acceptance of this new self that we find our true center, that place of quiet strength and solid being, that center from which we know and sell ourselves to be white-robed in the very righteousness of Christ himself.

The true self needs walking partners. One true word spoken by a brother or sister puts to flight a thousand rank ones. We need friends with "instructed tongues," those who listen in harmony with the Creator and Redeemer to speak the Word that sustains us in our weary forgetfulness (Isaiah 50:4).

Lucy called upon her friend when tempted by that familiar pattern of rejection; I am rescued frequently from the downdrag of emotions bound up by lies. When insecure in my masculinity, or tempted to define myself by the accusation of others, I call upon my wife or a comrade to remind me of something solid and true that endures in spite of the trial at hand.

Obviously, then, that real self is not a perfect self. An authentic self is just that—a person raised with Christ, born from above, who through God's mercy can admit what is still broken and needy about that self.

LIVING OUT LOUD

The authentic self does not carefully edit its offering in the hopes that others see only its strength and beauty. It knows too well that wounds and weakness can devolve into ugliness if not named and voiced. Raised with Christ, blessed and built up by others, the authentic self seeks trustworthy members of the community who can help remove the grave clothes that she or he still bears. Those grave clothes have names. It may be a profound area of wounding that one accepts as a healing in progress. What a gift to find those to whom one can submit the abuse, the abandonment, the betrayal.

Opened to the light of others' care, the wound heals more readily, and one is less apt to express the pain of it in destructive ways. We all have wounds, some that take a lot of time to heal. How blessed to be raised with Christ, his wounds yet visible. He thus frees us in turn to make visible our historic wounds to one another.

How difficult this can be. Yet the authentic self knows better than to suppress such wounds. What we won't express in the light will express itself darkly.

Rick grew up in a climate where a male homosexual (or anyone suspected of being one) was ridiculed, even threatened with violence. He learned to hide his same-sex attraction and his perceived weakness from anyone. When others surmised his "weakness," he felt exposed and went to lengths to deny their taunts.

He began to make efforts to relate openly with a few members of his community. He could tell one leader purposely avoided him and resisted calling him into further involvement. When Rick mishandled his short-lived friendship with a young woman, that leader was unusually harsh with him, and asked him to go to another small group. He accused Rick of being effeminate and not serious about God.

In truth, that leader had the problem—he was biased toward anyone who struggled with homosexuality. For Rick, it reopened a historic wound of rejection for his "difference." It apparently did not matter how hard he tried to live out God's will; to some like this man, he was still a flawed and perverse man. His wound tempted Rick to throw away his progress. He thought, *Why try? If the church just mirrors a biased world, then why not just go back to those who understand me and accept me?* One night, he drank too much wine. He felt like calling that old lover.

Then he thought about the good hard progress he had made, and of those trustworthy ones who stood with him in the process. He called the man walking with him in the healing process; he wept with Rick as Rick recounted the familiar accusing voice of the male leader. Rick wept. Therein lay his healing. He felt the real pain of living among cruel and biased people. Another suffered with him. He heard the words of a brother who reminded him of his true and solid masculine self, the real self Jesus had reclaimed in him, and how that self was stronger and more authoritative than the mere words of a man.

Related to wounds are our weaknesses. The authentic self knows it is weak; it has no illusion about strength apart from the merciful God. So the authentic self is quick to name that weakness so that the greater power may rest upon him or her. For some of us, that weakness can turn to wickedness unless it is named in a timely manner. That could have happened to Rick. Instead of pressing into the Body of Christ, he could have descended down the broad path of sexual immorality.

Only a few months later, he made such a descent. The next time I saw Rick, he was a mess. Ashamed and downcast, he could barely look at me. After holding strong for a while, he admitted that he fell back into a one-time sexual relation with his former "mentor." He explained it all, and I could see he was sick about his sin. He had been seduced by an older brother in Christ who was not ready or willing to face his own homosexuality; in truth, he had formed a relation with Rick based on sexual desire in the name of "discipleship." Rick saw the trouble only in part until the relationship became explicitly sexual.

It was a wake-up call for Rick. Having danced around the edges of a homosexual union, he fell in. But now he had tools— people who knew him and who stood with him in the truth of who he was and what he was committed to working out. He set a clear boundary with this man, and realized that they could go no further in any type of relationship. (The other was unrepentant and unwilling to submit to any process of restoration.)

Rick needed help to see that as terrible as this failure was, it was not the end of the healing process. Rather, it was a chance for his true self to rise and shine. He now had new authority to see the dangers outside himself and the weakness within; he could now make level paths for his feet. He was broken and humbled, but it was Jesus' opportunity, not the devil's.

His sexual failure was a wake-up call for him to enter into a new phase of his authentic self. He could shed some illusions about his own righteousness. Having sinned boldly, he could also apprehend the greater grace that rested upon him. Jesus was inviting him into a more genuine reliance upon himself and the community. To be weakened by hard knocks is human and invites us into deeper fellowship with him who became weak on our behalf.

In communion with him and his Body, love strengthens us where we are most in need of it. We make decisions in our weakness. We can submit humbly to help, or turn away to our own devices for coping with the weakness at hand. The latter constitutes wickedness—it is destructive to us and our most important relationships.

So to recap: the real self is the true, substantial self that Jesus has raised up from the dead of sin and separation from himself. That self requires that the community around us peel off the "grave clothes" we still wear upon emerging from the tomb (John 11:43-44). Like Lazarus, we need those disciples around us who obey Jesus' call to "unwrap" the newly raised self.

PROVOKING THE LION

Like most of us, Fernando was a paradox. On one hand, he was a quiet young man who strove to do the right thing. He tended more toward compliance and cooperation than asserting his own point of view. That was obvious in relation to Carmen. He adored her, and at first she appeared to dominate their relationship. Yet on the other hand, Fernando had an edge to him. He resented my counsel in one situation during a conference, and told me so plainly. While watching a sporting event on TV (broadcast during one of our gatherings), I could hear someone angrily screaming at the opposition then cheering for the home-team. It was Fernando!

The man had a bite, and I loved it. While praying for him, I blessed the powerful man that had not been declawed and de-tongued. Fernando was a lion whom God created to roar. I wanted to help him recover that roar in the best sense—to become fully alive to the power of his manhood in relation to God and others. That was a challenge for him. His family history of neglect, beginning with the early death of his mother, had left him untouched, with a huge unmet need for female bonding and touch. His father's critical voice without much ongoing care and discipline left him uncertain.

His early religious commitment gave life to him but failed to adequately engage his masculinity. The main symbols of the church tended to emphasize the weakness of Christ crucified and the feminine dimension of church through the Virgin Mary. He loved both, but he needed to be provoked and called out in his manhood. It did not happen in his early spiritual life. Sports provided some of that empowerment while Internet porn robbed him of power. His sin added guilt and shame to the mix of his masculine sexuality.

When he met Carmen, he adored her. He was drawn to her aloofness, and interpreted some of her contained beauty as a feminine virtue, highly spiritual. She was sexy yet virginal— all-good, slightly unattainable. In some ways, he had construed her as slightly surreal, an extension of his religious imagination. He served her slavishly but did not adequately engage with her as a valued counterpart; he needed to emerge into the reality of who she actually was, and who he was as one called to stand alongside of her as a powerful man.

He needed to find his voice in relation to her. He needed to realize that his masculine reality mattered to her and to the relationship. We talked about this as a couple. He felt inferior to her greater ease with words, and felt guilt over past failures with Internet porn. I asked Carmen to describe the ways that she loved and appreciated the strength Fernando brought into the relationship. She claimed she felt protected by him, and honored. She trusted him like no other. She wept, as no other knew her as he did and yet loved her.

I urged them both to establish a new commitment to sharing what they appreciated about the other and to honestly express their need for each other. Carmen admitted that she needed Fernando to initiate outrageous acts of kindness to her. She often felt as though he was a bit more like a child seeking to please a mother than a man asserting himself to a woman. That was a weakness for Fernando. He could not get from his wife what his mother would never be able to give him.

I knew he had it in him to relate to her as a grown man. "But what happens," I asked Fernando, "when you have initiated bold new things into the marriage?" "She rejects it on the basis that it's not what she wants." I brought up the possibility that his freedom to act could be choked out by her need for control. If he acted more freely toward her, could she flex and bless his effort?

Carmen admitted that her control was in part rooted in how his history of porn threatened her. It brought up her fears of abandonment (her father left the family for another woman).

That was an important insight for her. Carmen's weakness lay in transferring that threat of abandonment upon Fernando. "Do you really think he will leave you and the baby?" I asked.

She admitted it was an irrational fear, and that Fernando had demonstrated his trustworthiness. Yes Fernando had a weakness that could become wicked. Yet he was dealing with it responsibly with solid male friends. His struggle for purity did not invalidate the powerful good of his masculine sexuality and the way that he sought to love her through its expression. In giving her pleasure, he felt strong and virile, as if his manhood was a blessing, not a curse.

Both needed to demystify their sexual life together. Fernando needed to lay down that vision of Carmen as "the virgin queen."

Both agreed that her "control" was not a virtue but a defense against the threat of being rejected. These are very human responses to pain, not divine ones! Could she see his sexuality as a whole part of him through which he sought to love her, not use her? That was a challenge for her that she promised to consider.

Both had strengths. Carmen was a powerful, articulate and capable woman. She was a gift to Fernando and many others. Yet her weakness lay in using that strength as a defense against the reality that she was also very needy. In truth, she needed his masculine presence. Yet she was subject to burdening him with what he should not have to bear, namely, the sin of her father.

Fernando was a powerful sexual man, as well as a sensitive, considerate man. In turn, he had to own his weakness—how he tended to view Carmen as a mother, both spiritually and emotionally, when in truth she was merely a beautiful, flawed woman. She needed a whole man to help her recognize both. He in turn needed to refuse to make her something she was not.

What the one mirrored to the other was the way we carry our family wounds into our adult relationships. Both had made progress in recognizing "unfinished business": Fernando with the mother whose nurture he still longed for, Carmen with the father who abandoned the family. In facing the wound rightfully before God and others, each had the freedom to discover the spiritual healing Jesus offered them.

In the gaps, Jesus showed them the Father whose nurture and steadfast love pertained to their deepest needs. At the same time, these being-healed areas became a work in progress, rather than an underlying current of expectation or resentment in their marriage. Secure in their authentic selves, they began to accept graciously their weak tendencies in relation to each other. Through grace, each could begin to make different choices. Fernando began to initiate new expressions of love and so further prevail over any false images he held. She in turn began to release some of her need for control and learn to welcome this man's earnest efforts to love her more authentically than he had before.

FALSE FRONTS

Once while praying for Rick, I had a picture of the interior of a house. At first it appeared to be in order. All the furniture was in place, well-coordinated, pleasing to the eye. That was obvious of the man in general—he presented well, and possessed a kind of ease and charm that set others at ease. But in the picture, I saw that the house was not set on the solid ground, but on blocks of earth above ground that were crumbling. I could see that one end of the house was actually beginning to sink as the blocks eroded. My hunch? Rick needed help to identify what was lacking in some foundational areas of his life. I knew that God would help us to get there in time.

Rick had grown up without much masculine input at all. His father had been a well-known missionary, much admired in his local community, but gone most of the time. He died when Rick, his only son, was young. Rick's mother had relied upon him in her grief and need. He loved her a lot, but also felt pressure to be something for her that he could not fulfill adequately. Living in a tight religious culture sometimes added to that pressure; Rick had little room to be the sinner that he was.

So his presentation was not wholly in line with the crumbling realities under the surface. He knew he needed so much, but struggled to admit that he was broken. He was eager to serve, but I sensed that such service was part of his "religious self," the boy who did all things well but was not free to have need. I spoke into the solid ground of his masculinity. I told him what I saw: not crumbling blocks but real solid ground that Jesus had won for him on the cross. Until he actually discovered that ground and could rest upon it, I told him that he would keep striving to invite people into a "house" that was subject to breaking down, buckling under the weight of his weakness, as it had with his sexual failure.

He needed to know that Jesus had taken that ground for him already. Yes, he had much to work out to actually discover that ground for himself. His father had left Rick a legacy without the gift of imparting that legacy through an ongoing relationship. I asked him about his father, what he knew of him. What I knew of Rick seemed to line up with aspects of what he described about his father: faith, perseverance, a spirit of adventure and conquest. I urged him onward with the truth of how Jesus wanted him to be united with the good inheritance he had received from his father.

Jesus brought the gift of his Father to Rick. United with him, Rick is discovering afresh the living, breathing life-giving aspects of his manhood that had been dormant. He possesses the goods, and Jesus' is intent on reclaiming for him what had been lost in his father's absence. I loved this man and I expressed it. I told him: "If I care for you as I do, knowing the precious and profane truths that I now know, how much more does Jesus?"

Jesus has raised Rick from the dead; he has given him new ground on which to stand in his masculinity. But in order for Christ's resurrection (and Rick's, in Christ) to have its full benefit, Rick must do his part. Rick can stand in the authentic self. In that self, he can stay honest with a couple of others about his "father-wound" and the way he sometimes aches for masculine touch and attention. Submitting his homosexual tendencies to good brothers is key; he need not allow weakness to become once more a stronghold of wickedness. In truth, his need can become an invitation for real, substantial love.

FORSAKING FALSE REFUGE

Lucy had made such progress. She was like a plant deprived of nutrients who flourished upon receiving them. It was easy to identify and call out the beautiful woman who was emerging out of the tomb of isolation and rejection. Not only had she significantly shed the grave clothes of fearing men and her need for them, she was beginning to grow and learn through different relationships with them. I was and am one of them!

Still, she tended to overly spiritualize her life. Sometimes it was hard to get a straight answer from her—she would respond to questions about her well-being with a Scripture or vision. I would then gently say: "I am talking to you, the human being, not the 'spirit-being.'"

While praying for her, I received a picture of herself, her "home," if you will. Like Rick's, it was in good order, but there was a wing of the house that was markedly different from the other rooms. It seemed like it had been created hastily and without the proper plan or building code—though clean, it had a childish unreality to it—youthful posters depicting icons of popular culture. I asked her if that made any sense to her. She admitted that it was the room of her youth, the place of escape from the hard realities of her childhood.

She told me of her military father who could be harsh and cruel to all, especially Lucy's mother. She admitted to the frightening battles her parents would have, with her mother sobbing and her father stomping off. Lucy would then escape into her room. Her fervent faith now composed the basis for her new reality, one far from the hard realities of her family of origin.

Lucy's weakness lay in her still wanting to use alternative realities as a way of avoiding the pain of her life. I urged her to make peace with pain, how it pointed to real injuries that Jesus wanted to heal. Jesus redeems our suffering; he does not give us an escape from it. Only though identification with the Crucified and his Father—both wounded by the vast distance they experienced from one another at Calvary—could Lucy find a place to go with her sorrow. And only through resurrection— the powerful reunion between Father and Son—could Lucy be assured that healing would result from submitting her wounds to Jesus and others.

Lucy tearfully admitted the fear she had toward the cruelty of her father toward her mother, and the resentment she held toward her mother for just taking it. She also admitted that she wanted to avoid her family altogether. She was part of a new spiritual family now—she lived in a new town, with new friends, and a new spiritual community. "Why dredge up the past?" she asked.

I urged her to consider how much she was like them, having been sourced in the soil of a particular marriage and family. Now that she had the grace to extend to them, she might be rightfully reconciled with her "source," humanly speaking. She began to see how walling off from painful relationships had not stopped the pain; it just walled her off from relationships in general.

Forgiveness took on new meaning for Lucy. Like many Christians, Lucy had leaped over her painful past with one broad jump of forgiveness. In truth, her pardon meant little as she had never faced the actual wounds she still bore.

I introduced a new concept for her: the sin of misogyny, or the dishonor of women. Lucy grew up in a culture and a home where women were subject to men in ways that dishonored them. Her mother had been subject to her husband's rough and demanding way toward his wife, especially when he drank. Lucy shuddered still at frightening memories of disrespect in her parents' marriage. Lucy's mother rarely stood up for herself.

For this, Lucy felt both pity and disdain for her: pity because of her dishonor, and disdain because she allowed herself to be dishonored. Mom and Dad were both misogynists; they danced in dishonor. Conflicted, Lucy walled herself off from the whole family.

The true self has power to identify the wall and deconstruct it, one well-aimed act of forgiveness at a time. Lucy began a series of such acts, forgiving her parents for their misogyny from her heart. That is how Jesus frees us from the sin of our forefathers—not through denial, but through facing it at the cross. Only there can dishonor find an end. Only there can our hearts be free for the honor he wants for us.

She took these words seriously, and committed to walk them out. In order for Lucy to continue to forsake her tendency to deny pain through overly spiritualizing things, she had to face the pain of her life. She also needed partnerships. I urged her to press into the relationships in her community that would help her face pain honestly before Jesus and under the power of his cross. The cross thus took on a new communal dimension for Lucy; it became a place of refuge for her.

HOME FOR HEALING

Bev needed the healing of misogyny at an even deeper level. Perhaps the most profound expression of misogyny is the sexual abuse of female children. Bev's uncle should have used his greater power to confirm her femaleness; instead, he defiled it. The fact that Bev's mother refused to believe her daughter was another layer of misogyny. Her mom perpetuated the false system of honor that protects the most powerful one, in this case, the uncle. She unwittingly conveyed to her daughter that dishonoring women is a fact of life for which there is no justice. That Bev's whole family was "Christian" only added to the nightmare for her. In truth, Bev was not yet free to go home. But where a mother and father might forsake her, the Lord would receive her (Psalm 27:10).

God knew what he was doing in bringing up these issues in that season. The time had not been right before. Her support system was not yet in place. Now, Bev was ready; she was surrounded by people who loved her well and within certain limits. A long-term healing group, a counselor, a church that supports such healing and some friends were standing with her. Raised with Christ, her wounds yet visible to the community, Bev was ready to let us help her remove the "grave clothes" of another's perversion.

Bev held fast to Psalm 18:16-19; these words mattered to her deeply:

> He reached down from on high and took hold of me;
>> he drew me out of deep waters.
> He rescued me from my powerful enemy,
>> from my foes, who were too strong for me.
> They confronted me in the day of my disaster,
>> but the LORD was my support.
> He brought me out into a spacious place;
>> he rescued me because he delighted in me.

That passage spoke to Bev of God's sovereign hand; he had removed her from both the falsehood in her family and false ways of coping with the pain in a string of lesbian relationships. It also spoke to her of God setting her in a spacious, well-defined place. There she was beginning to examine the damage done and receive the Lord's honor at the deepest level possible.

In order to be redeemed, deep wounds like childhood sexual abuse require a context. Until that context is properly in place, it is unwise to dabble with the fragile soul at hand. Yet with a community committed to a deep healing process, the wounded one discovers afresh the strength of resurrection. Raised with Christ in his body, one is then free to suffer redemptively—to access the injury, receive healing and let go of the grave clothes that defined one's wounded life.

For Bev, that involved returning to the memory of those sexual crimes. With sensitive guidance from prayer counselors, she received Jesus' help where it was most urgently needed. She sobbed as she hadn't sobbed before, and received his advocacy and his washing as she had never received before. She realized that the perversion she bore in her depths was not hers but another's; she allowed Jesus to bear it all. He crowned her with honor.

I began to see a sweet and childlike quality in Bev I had not seen before. I realized that her childhood had been significantly extinguished by the abuse. "Struck down," I thought, "but not destroyed" (2 Corinthians 4:9). Jesus began to revive the child who lay dormant, awaiting spring. In the light and warmth of his community, Bev began to trust others; she began to open and marvel at the beauty of love that surrounded her. A hard, angry quality in her gave way to gratitude. We who stood with Bev had the privilege to glimpse this awakening. And to speak out and bless the wonder of innocence restored—the childlike component of her authentic self.

In the process, she identified the manipulation and control that she had exercised to meet her needs relationally. She coped with the abuse by exerting a kind of infantile control over others.

Seeing it clearly, she sought to repent of this. She now saw some of the inner logic for the boundaries her friends had set with her. Having her boundaries violated so basically, she realized it would take some time to rebuild them. She had faith to do so. She was learning to trust.

It has been beautiful to behold her emergence. We are seeing Lazarus alive and well and progressively free from her grave clothes. Through her suffering and healing, Bev remarked that she has had the privilege through her suffering to discover her own theology of crucifixion and resurrection. And she is witnessing a flowering of gifts—eyes of faith with which to see others restored, and a gift of faith for God to increase the spacious place of her church's healing community.

She has a long way to go. The wounds are deep, the healing an equally profound and lengthy process. She is still weak in her boundaries and still prone to manipulation and control. His grace is greater still through the community that surrounds her.

Through this process, all involved are invited to discover the wonder and marvel and challenge of Paul's words when he says, "I want to know Christ and the power of his resurrection and the fellowship of sharing in his suffering, becoming like him in his death, and so, somehow, to attain to the resurrection from the dead" (Philippians 3:10-11).

God raised Bev from the dead of dishonor in order to crown her with honor. He used his Body to do so, fulfilling Paul's description to the Corinthians that God had already extended "greater honor to the parts [of the body] that lacked it" (1 Corinthians 12:24).

No stranger to how he had dishonored others, Jake was beginning to discover the depth of his own need for healing. His sin was the most obvious of the six; his wounds were not. Not even to himself. As a traditional guy, fortified by macho culture, there was little value ascribed to facing his wounds. Wounds were feminine; wounds were "weakness." To Jake, real guys fought hard, and just kept fighting.

I could see how getting on a serious track for sobriety in the sexual arena had humbled him. He was working the program; he had gotten serious with God about the effects of his sin upon others. One would be hard pressed to not see the fruit of repentance growing in him. And yet I could also see that he had little insight into any way that he had been damaged by others. He owned his sin. Even that gave him a kind of control; he had done devilish things to women; he repented, he worked the program. His heart remained contained, closed off. Something was missing.

God gave me faith for Jake's whole authentic self. He shied away from me a bit. He had problems with guys like me coming out of homosexuality. I did not take offense. I pressed into relationship with him because God gave me a view of his heart. I could see that at the core he possessed a sensitive heart. He hated that in himself. I knew that his owning that heart was key to him truly loving others well.

I had a picture for him of his heart. It was big and open and tender. And it had a tear in it that ran down the middle. I thought of Ezekiel's words when he prophesied that God would cleanse us of all impurity and would remove the heart of stone and give us a heart of flesh, a heart capable of deep feeling, able to respond to God's passionate will for us (Ezekiel 36:25-26).

Jake learned in Living Waters about various types of abuse; the teacher concretely described the various expressions of how adults sexually abuse children, including fondling, sex talk, and lustful looks and intentions. Jake came to me afterward and wanted to talk. He described haltingly how an aunt who took care of him during his late childhood and early teen years abused him. He never saw it as such. Mentally unstable, she would make comments about his sexuality, touch him and insinuate herself on him. To him, she was a confusing, strange woman, and he just steeled himself from her during their time together.

In truth, she had violated him and he defended himself behind a stony wall of "real men take it and move on." But he had not moved on. He was harassed by memories of the scary look in her eye and the dread of her actions. He bore humiliation and anger, even rage, at what she had done—a woman violating a man. He hated her for making him weak, and vowed never to let that happen to him again. He had successfully lived out that vow in his misuse of women as an adult. In his immorality, he controlled the sensual acts and kept them far from his heart. He was beginning to recognize how he hurt women. God was giving him a new opportunity to recognize that hurt in himself.

Abuse is an equal opportunity offender. Female abuse of boys is humiliating, confusing and disempowering. Without healing, one is subject to avoidance and/or aggressive acts against women later in life. God was giving Jake a heart of flesh.

He needed room to feel the pain of his life. He did it his way. I never saw him break down and sob or vent his rage dramatically. He bore his pain differently than more expressive ones. But he discovered a new facet of Jesus: not only the lamb who takes away the sins he committed, but the sins committed against him.

Jake had gotten used to Jesus' just anger at his offenses toward women. He was now becoming tenderized by the Lamb's passion for his suffering—the justice of the Crucified toward the crucifying effects of his own abuse. Softened by such mercy, he began to identify the core misogyny in his heart. His dishonor of women was more than cultural; it was also his reaction to having been dishonored by women.

That reaction took some time to disassemble; the process included forgiving his abuser from the heart, while exercising the truth that women were his equals and deserving of respect. In the process, I could see God awakening Jake's "heart of flesh." Having raised Jake from the dead, Jesus was intent on using all things—including his wounds and weakness, to make Jake more like himself. He was intent on making Jake a man capable of empathy and profound sensitivity. He was becoming a man who could love others well.

Maybe that's the point: Jesus frees us to bear with him our wounds and weaknesses. In so doing we become authentically human. Like him, raised from the dead, we yet bear the mark of our brokenness and are thus able to bear with others in theirs. Having received mercy in profound and often shameful areas, we can draw from our personal "well" to extend mercy to loved ones.

The authentic self makes peace with its brokenness. It is not defined by an absence of wounds or weakness or failure. Its inspired quality lies in how readily that self admits to any of the three. Why? As Paul implores us, it is so that Christ's mercy and power may rest more thoroughly upon it (2 Corinthians 12:7-10).

A good reflection of wholeness is how well you deal with your brokenness.

COMMUNITY PROPERTY

In order to mature in love, the authentic self must also take seriously its call to community. Our flaws are community property! The candor with which we convey our "incompleteness" invites partnership. Not that others exist to be our answer. Rather, trusted ones bear witness of the greater life—the everlasting mercy—that is our answer. That could become an exercise in self-indulgence if we did not take seriously our call to do the same for our community partners. The authentic self is not a mere child before merciful parents.

While we bear weakness, deeper still is the sustaining mercy that must be activated and stirred up by releasing it to others. Knowing one's need, while simultaneously offering oneself as a gracious witness of the merciful One, is a mark of the authentic self.

My recovery from homosexual addiction made me the more obvious "sinner" in my marriage. But Annette had comparable wounds and weaknesses. However quiet her wounds and weakness were publicly, they were loud in our intimate relationship. God in his mercy freed Annette to admit them, and I learned to receive that offering as a gift. It can be tough for us at times. Yet such bearing with each other's brokenness unites us in mercy. We brought brokenness into the marriage and marriage did not cure it. Rather, marriage exposed the brokenness and changed us as we learned to bear with one another mercifully.

All six of our friends were united in a commitment to this authentic self and to relationships founded on that type of "reality." They had experienced too much grace to not want to offer the whole self to others, and to have reasonable expectation that their close partnerships might share a comparable freedom of expression. They needed that. Without "talking" partners, all six could be subject to the weakness that becomes wicked, even diabolical, in close friendships.

A personal example might help. One night, after a church meeting that had tough implications for Annette's and my future, I immediately went into a tailspin. Yet I worked hard to deny it. On the drive home, I was besieged with all my worst temptations—chemical, sexual, relational—in that I became critical and intolerant. Still, when Annette asked, I insisted that the meeting went OK and "could we talk about it later?" She saw right through it, and gently asked me what actually happened.

That was my invitation: to tell the truth and so be spared the sinful expression of my wound. To keep lying only enhanced the options crouching at my door. I have a good partner. I haltingly laid it all out. She began to cry, and together we faced the difficulty at hand and awaited the merciful One. We felt the pain together; we were united in our common wound. We did not know the way forward but could agree that he is the way and that he would change us as we waited together. He did. That wound made us more whole because of our freedom of expression, our faith in his mercy and his faithfulness to spare us from sin when we express our pain rightfully to each other.

François Fénelon writes: "When you feel your heart sinking under trouble, be simple and frank in saying so. Don't be ashamed to let your weakness be seen, or to ask for help in your urgent need. So doing you will advance in simplicity, in humility and trustfulness." Perhaps that is the strength of the authentic self. It makes the need known, be it a wound, a weakness, a failure or just one's need of another. And that self seeks out others who do the same. The result? Relationships built on humility and trust.

God mercifully indwells such unions and frees us to be deep wells of that mercy for each other.

8

HOME ALONE

HOW THE PRACTICE OF SOLITUDE
PREPARES US FOR OTHERS

My house will be called a house of prayer.

MATTHEW 21:13

God created us for relationships. That is the essence of our sexual longing—the urge to yield up the walls of our house in order to merge with another. Fruitfulness—the capacity to create new life—requires such a joint enterprise. We may struggle as we aspire "to not be alone." Yet we thrive when activated by that hearty, bodily longing. God made us that way. It is good (Genesis 2:18).

Yet arguably, togetherness draws meaning and vitality from solitude. One's strength of relating to another will be founded on the depth of his or her intimacy with God. I am convinced that we join best with others when we have quieted the clamor of our longings for them. Alone before God, we discover the wellspring of life that waters our efforts to be a good gift. We arise, sobered and enlivened by Christ, the love that makes all things new.

Could it be that the God who created us for others uses the perils of human relating to draw us nearer to himself? The road to intimacy with others is a delightful one, but also thorny and painfully revealing, as we have seen with our six friends. Others provoked wounds, weakness and wickedness in them; at other times, mere need. Yet even the summoning of pure need in another grants no guarantee that a mere human can satisfy that need, not in full anyway.

HUNGRY FOR GOD

Other humans are ready targets for our hungers. In solitude, God calls us away from that "din of desire" and back to himself. There we await "the still small voice" once the storm and wind and quaking motions of our souls have passed (1 Kings 19:12). Solitude is desert-like. Far from the roar of many desires and distractions, we hunger. In the desert, God humbles us and feeds us his way. He weans us from the bread others give us and teaches us afresh through the words of his mouth (Deuteronomy 8:3).

In the early days of my recovery, I began the good habit of committing to a couple of friends for prayer, accountability and just plain connecting with guys because I need them. One day, I was really struggling. I felt alone, sexually aroused and hungry for relationship. Neither of my pals was available. I was mad. "OK, here I am, doing the right thing and no one is there for me. Maybe I'll masturbate or hook up with someone. That'll show 'em." (As if my moral failure would be a punishment for them.)

Then I felt that prompting—the still small voice. I realized I needed God. He was there. He could satisfy me. I released my lustful desires to him and reeled in the loose wires lashing out at my friends; I quieted my heart. I recited words of comfort from the Psalms that I had hidden in my heart. I cried because of his mercy, and then I cried more because his kindness frees me to face real hardship the right way: on my knees.

That was a hard season of life for me. God made that season fruitful by his faithful love for me. At times that love came through people; at other times, through his presence alone.

The symbol of the cross helps me a lot in solitude. It frees me to behold the Lord of mercy. His mercy liberates my surrender. The cross then gathers my thoughts and desires and urges me to surrender them afresh to that mercy. It reminds me that my well-being hinges upon that surrender. And the well-being of others who get bit or slimed when I am not bridled by mercy! All other desires must bow before him in order for mercy to transform me.

My prayer time is fairly simple and easy to emulate. I begin by letting random thoughts and desires of the preceding day come up and out before him. I no longer am shocked by my murderous or defiling fountain. I just trust in God—the Source that surpasses my filth. I often behold myself at the mouth of some ancient spring. Its waters whisk away the debris from my heart; I simply trust the "crosscurrent" to cleanse what is foul and replenish what is true. I await that living water at the cross, confident that he works in me as I rest in him.

I meditate on Scripture. (Once a week, I take a longer time and commit to memory an extended passage that I then bring to mind in this daily time.) I pray for the few people that I commit to pray for daily. I lift up unexpected needs. Mostly I just rest in his mercy. The cross reminds me that he has done it. For me, for us all. I rest in that. I need its cleansing, healing waters daily. I don't want to draw life from anything else.

Things become clear while resting. Prayer for me is the spacious, well-lit place where I see things I don't normally see in the bustling hours, especially about my sexuality or relationships. I may observe in prayer inordinate thoughts toward a particular person. Maybe I have made another an idol, given him or her too much power to bless or curse me. I surrender those inklings to God before they become a stronghold.

Maybe I am sensitized in quiet to the needs of my wife, and in turn I am alerted to our need for greater connection. Maybe I am alerted to my need for male friendship. I listen for the hungers and submit them to God, trusting that he will guide me as I arise from prayer and engage in life-giving ways with others.

TRANSFORMATION

In solitude, our human hungers become converted from lust to normal longings. We can learn to manage them well once the Creator has become the center of our affections and will. Leanne Payne writes of this conversion beautifully:

> Every one of us—not just those who are the most visibly wounded by the darkness in humanity and the world—has to face the inner loneliness. . . . We all need to begin the rigorous but sternly magnificent work of converting the "desert of loneliness" within into the spaciously beautiful "garden of solitude" where the true self comes forward and flourishes. This is the self capable of friendship and Christian fellowship. Its identity is no longer in the creature. It no longer demands that the creature to be god to it.

I am convinced that all of us need to face that loneliness before God. Relational wounds, disappointments, and expectancies need to be faced before the Lord. There we are reminded that he alone is our anchor, sure and steadfast (Hebrews 6:19). He alone is constant amid the "rising and falling of many" relationships that we face this side of heaven. We discover Christ as the ballast of our intrepid, often battered, vessel; we discover Christ as the harbor within which we are refurbished for the journey at hand. He transforms loneliness into solitude.

Henri Nouwen writes knowingly of solitude and healthy relationships:

> Without solitude, we begin to cling to each other; we begin to worry about what we think and feel about each other; we quickly become suspicious of one another or irritated with one another; we begin, often in unconscious ways, to scrutinize each other with a tiring hypersensitivity. Without solitude, shallow conflicts easily grow deep and cause painful wounds. Then "talking things out" can become a burdensome obligation and daily life so self-conscious that long-term living together is virtually impossible. . . . With solitude, however, we learn to depend on God, by whom we are called together in love, in whom we can rest, and through whom we can enjoy and trust one another even when our ability to express ourselves to each other is limited. With solitude, we are protected against the harmful effect of mutual suspicions, and our words and actions can become joyful expressions of an already existing trust rather than a subtle way of asking for proof of trustworthiness. With solitude we can experience each other as different manifestations of a love that transcends us all.

God wants us. As Creator, he wants our worship. He will not allow us to make gods and goddesses of mere creatures. As Redeemer, he wants to be the foundation on which we grow in love with others. He wants to be the love from which our human loves find meaning and achieve the purpose for which he intended them.

To be sure, human relationships can be conduits of divine love for us. Yet as Nouwen astutely observes, these created sources of grace stay clear and free for us when we rightly draw from the Source himself. We simply tend to make the creature what she or he cannot be—divine.

Solitude that invites intimacy with God frees us to surrender such idolatry and so liberate the creature to be merely created, a limited conduit of love. Then, filled afresh with his Spirit, we are able to draw from the good gifts others can give and navigate gracefully the regrettable offerings we may receive from them!

My need for same-sex intimacy was intense at the beginning of my healing journey. When I would allow myself to need the one or two brothers I actually trusted, the need was overwhelming. My unmet needs resulted in inordinate expectations of my friends. I would begin to get jealous of how they spent their time, and whether or not I felt like I was a priority to them. I was miserable, and beginning to make them miserable. I came to my senses and realized that I was vulnerable to making them gods—my primary source of life. I had bypassed God for them. I was no longer "sourced" in God and grateful for these secondary sources. Mere created beings had become primary to me and I in turn resented them for not assuaging my loneliness.

It was a painful but swift repentance. I returned to my knees before the source of unfailing love and gave my friends space and grace to give what they could. My repentance saved those friendships and taught me an abiding truth that became foundational to my marriage. Obviously, marriage is about two becoming one—there is freedom for a depth of mutual reliance that one might not expect in friendship. Yet marriage itself can become a source of idolatry. Whenever one relies upon a marital partner as the *basis* for one's identity and well-being, they cast a shadow on God.

I saw this in several ways: Annette relying on me to give her what only God could, my failure to endure tension between us that I knew would take time to work out, our struggle to turn to God to give us grace to accept our unified life and calling together. When these things manifested, it became quickly apparent to us: we both need God to be God, the primary source of our well-being. Needing the other badly and frustrated at the perceived lack, fretting about the gaps in our connection— these were life-signs that directed us back to God. The essence of Payne's and Nouwen's words gave life to us; they reminded us that God is our Savior and there is no other.

KEY TO LOVING WELL

Solitude is a key to being replenished in love so we can love others better. He wants us to approach them with gratitude, extending an open hand and heart to the beautifully imperfect gift before us. In solitude he meets us in quiet, even imperceptible ways. Like an unseen river overflowing its banks and leaving behind nutrients on the dry soil, his Spirit saturates us as we abide in his love.

No culture or personality is exempt from the call to solitude. Jesus pulled away from the crowds in order to hear the Father's voice. So must we. Indeed, we face uneasiness in addressing the unseen God. We feel acutely our aloneness in solitude. The noise within is louder when we are alone. We may clamor for sensual connection when we unplug. We are wired that way.

Gerald May writes, "When people tell me they have trouble taking time for prayer and meditation, I often ask them what unpleasant things they might be wanting to avoid." Yet deeper even than our avoidance is our longing for the tender and strong

One. When I first brought up the call to devotional solitude to our six friends, four looked away. The other two rolled their eyes. They had heard it all before—the "quiet time" that never happens, the dusty (and complicated) prayer notebook with few enthusiastic entries, the elusive "passion" of prayer.

I urged them to reconsider devotionals as a time to enter the rest of his presence. Rather than a task, God was calling them back into the water, back to mercy. I love those verses from Hebrews 4:9-11 that speak of a sabbath-rest for God's people: "Let us, therefore, make every effort to enter that rest, so that no one will fall by following their [the faithless, grumbling Hebrews on the desert] example of disobedience" (Hebrews 4:11).

It does take a little effort. But the effort is unto rest, refueling, a gentle sorting out before the loving God that prepares us for loving others. I tend toward a daily hour of just being before him, focusing simply on the cross, or a Scripture committed to memory, or simply a word—"mercy" or "come rest," for example—breathed in on the first word or syllable, exhaled on the second. I am weary most of the time when I pray, so I long for his love just to make me new, to help me to love others well.

Deal gently with the rubble which surfaces in solitude—the distracting, disturbing thoughts that go unnoticed in "civilian" life. Remember, it's about surrender to the One who takes our offering (however pathetic) cleanses us, then prepares us in love for the new day.

If an hour seems too long, start with fifteen minutes. Just take the time for abiding in him. Turn off the screens, unplug the ear-phones. Get quiet and turn toward the God who has already turned toward us. Jim Borst describes beautifully such contemplation: "The lips and mind both come to rest; there is a simple gazing at the Lord, where the heart reaches out without words and the will seeks to be one with God's will. Contemplation is the awareness of God, known and loved at the core of one's being."

I often see these few minutes as sinking into God, the source. Instead of revving up for a spiritual battle or exercise, it's about resting and receiving afresh what he has won for us. Then I am better able to extend myself generously to others, based upon his awesome and generous love for me.

All six agreed to take a portion of time alone each day and just *be* before the Lord. I followed up with them in subsequent meetings to help each evaluate the effects of solitude, and maximize its benefits.

SURFACING FEAR

For Bev, being alone could be fearful. She struggled "to abide." Memories and emotions of abuse sometimes arose in silence, and made it hard for her to trust and rest in God. In pain, she tended to race to people—important but limited due to the limits of mediators. I helped her to reconsider her time of solitude. I asked her to consider verses and a picture or object that helps to convey Jesus to her. She listed a few passages and brought out a beautiful cross on which Jesus' arms were extending upward in a powerful, healing way.

What a dynamic expression of Christ crucified and resurrected! I encouraged her to make the cross of Christ a focal point. That give her an outlet for the pain that continued to surface for an extended season. She was learning to abide with Christ in her suffering, knowing that he bore it with her and remained with her in it.

I urged her to do something I have learned to do when working out my wounding before God. When the pain starts coming up, get comfortable. Focus on Christ and his work on the cross. In his death, he descended into the depths of abuse;

and he rose again to raise us up and out of it. Place the cross on the heart as a physical representation of Christ's cross and make known your pain to him. Let the ache flow into his wounding. Let God gather up those emotions and unite them with Christ himself. Let him bear the unbearable. That's why he came—to bear the power of sin. Abuse was a sin imposed by another. Let him have it.

In solitude, Bev would begin to feel the ache. She would have flashbacks but I urged her to simply let them rise up and find their end in Christ. Bearing the cross on her chest, she would focus on Christ's cross and let God suffer with her. She began to realize that she was not alone in her pain—another suffered with and for her.

Bev began to look forward to her secret time with Christ crucified and raised. The Holy Spirit gave her pictures: one was of a large wound decreasing in size each time she offered it to Christ. Sometimes she felt a lot of emotion, sometimes just a dull aching reminder of the abuse. But every time she offered her wound to Jesus, she grew in intimacy with him. She trusted him more and more each time. She began to realize that her most profound wound had power, once submitted to Christ, to make her more whole.

The key to this wholeness was forgiveness. On one occasion, I asked her to begin to incorporate forgiving her abuser after she had poured out her thoughts and emotions to Jesus. I urged her to surrender her uncle to the Lord, to let Jesus serve justice his way. I urged her to give him that authority that she would not spend needless time and energy worrying about her abuser's punishment.

She began to release mercy to the man who had hurt her most; she also began to release mercy to her parents for not stopping the abuse. She especially had to forgive her mother for denying it even happened. Bev needed a lot of time to hurt and forgive at the cross. In time, she began to feel lighter. And to engage a bit more freely with others in her community: mostly women, but a few men as well. She would emerge from solitude more willing to engage with others. And yet she remained cautious.

A new fear emerged. Without the heaviness of the wound and the decrease of her own defensive reactions, she now felt more vulnerable to others, and that included the threat of more abuse from men and a heightened temptation to eroticize women. I assured her that each time she had let down the wall of her defense and allowed Jesus into her wound, she honored him as her refuge and fortress, her defensive wall, if you will. He was becoming her protector. Another dwelled with her; she did not relate to others alone.

I shared with her this vision that God gave me some years before. It helped her. It did not take away all the fear, but it gave her courage to go forward into new relationships on trembling legs and an increasingly whole heart.

JESUS AS REFUGE

The picture began with Jesus peering over a wall and spotting a child hiding in its long shadow. Jesus asked if he could come over, and with the child's assent, Jesus came over the wall and—with his back against the wall, facing the child—asked her what happened. She recounted the injury, tearfully, and she saw tears flowing from his eyes. "I've known betrayal too," he said, revealing his nail-scarred hands. "But my wounds have a purpose, to grant your wounds a healing place. Press your wounds into mine. Let me bear the wound and wounder. Let me be the one who serves justice. As you forgive, entrusting destiny to me, poison flows from your broken heart into mine.

I can take it. And I will cover your weakened heart—I will be its healer."

As the child embraces Jesus, she presses her wounded heart into his. "Even as Christ forgave me, so I forgive this one for hurting me so," says the child. Darkness flows from her and into Christ. Love, joy, and peace flow from Christ into the child. Stepping back, the child looks and notices that the wall is gone. All that stands is Christ—her sole defense.

Jesus says, "See through my eyes the one who wounded you." Know that I stand as your mediator, your protection, your defense. No one has power anymore to master you through their sin because your life is bound up in my life. You can absolutely count on my unfailing love for you. No matter what broken people do to you, I prevail over sin and its power to prevail over you."

SOLITUDE IN MARRIAGE

Fernando and Carmen each needed to find the cross in solitude. Aloneness brought up different fears in each of them. Fernando actually had to face the fact that he had made his wife an idol of sorts. In his loneliness and significant "mother-wound," he had depended on her too much. Separation from her felt terrifying to him—not just the normal sadness but almost a threat to his very sense of being.

Solitude also brought up pornographic temptations—a grasping after comfort in mere images. I urged him to simply wait before the Lord as those desires came up, not to suppress but rather to release them to his cleansing flood. Beneath them lay an older ache tied to his mother's early death and alcoholism. He needed to find Jesus as his comfort. I gave to him these words that Moses gave the tribe of Benjamin: "Let the beloved of the LORD rest secure in him, for he shields him all day long, and the one the LORD loves rests between his shoulders" (Deuteronomy 33:12).

Fernando needed solitude in order to allow Jesus to be for him what no mere human could be. His soul's transformation from desert to garden was marked by fits and starts. He persevered because he loved Jesus and wanted him above all else. He clung to his cross—its full power to bind him to the Father's shoulders whether he felt those shoulders or not. Sometimes he did. The peace and release of longing in his presence was delightful. At other times he just clung and derived meaning from the encounter by faith alone.

He began to see that Carmen could not make up for his "mother-wound." It was unfair to make her something she was not. She was not his mother. Nor was she his Savior. He needed solitude in order to remind himself that though they were one, they were also people separate from each other. Marriage did not negate the need to draw ultimate meaning from their Source; marriage necessitated that need for Jesus. Especially in light of the misbegotten motives that had fueled some of his bond with her.

Carmen, on the other hand, needed solitude to sort out the pain she felt from Fernando's porn weakness. It cut deep. Not because he was such a chronic "user"; his habit was in fact relatively light, and he was responsibly bringing it under control with male accountability partners. The problem lay in what his weakness provoked in her: her "father-wound"—the man who left her as a child for another woman.

That wound fueled a semi-irrational rage over Fernando's failures. She honestly thought she could not cope if he ever returned to porn. (This was after an extended time of victory on his part!) She angrily announced to Fernando during a session with me that if he ever looked at any porn image again she would leave him. We heard her out. I urged her to consider whether it was wise to base her whole commitment to Fernando

on whether he ever looked at another flickering image. I asked
her to take a day and reconsider that requirement.

It needs to be clear that there are valid reasons for separating from a spouse, for example, if Fernando was unrepentant
and unaccountable in areas of sexual sin and thus subjecting
the household to real darkness. That was not the case here.
Fernando's weakness was actually provoking a deeper fear in
Carmen. In solitude, she faced that fear. She clung to the cross
and asked Jesus to be her protector from the threat of infidelity. She felt so naked and vulnerable in that moment. It was the
little girl looking for a guarantee that a man would not hurt her
again.

I urged her to see the cross as the necessary dividing line
between herself and Fernando. I urged her to also see the cross
as that which pulls up the divisions, and makes them a whole
unit (Ephesians 2:14-16). I asked her if she could trust Jesus
with her marriage, even if she could not trust Fernando.

She had more grief to pour out at the cross. Fernando's
weakness brought up old wounds provoked by the wickedness of her father. She needed to understand the difference
between the two. And how bearing with a man in his weakness was not a one-time, "it's all over now" proposition. She
could choose (or not) to bear with Fernando because Jesus
does, and in Christ she could be empowered to entrust her
husband to his recovery.

That involved understanding her husband as a man who possessed both strengths and weaknesses. Could she rejoice in the
former and persevere with him in the latter? I encouraged her with
some words about the cross and perseverance from Bonhoeffer:

> Perseverance, translated literally, means: remaining un-
> derneath, not throwing off the load, but bearing it. We

know too little in the church about the peculiar blessing of bearing. Bearing, not shaking off but not collapsing either; bearing as Christ bore the cross, remaining underneath, and there beneath it—to find Christ.

I asked her to consider this, to determine whether she would accept this cross: the reality that her husband bore real moral weakness. She wondered whether or not she was setting herself up for rejection.

I highlighted again the big difference between weakness and wickedness: if Fernando had been justifying his sin and failing to get the help he needed, yes, she would be foolish to persevere in blind faith. She would have been enabling his wickedness. But actually he was working hard to stay clean. That hard effort was his cross—persevering in God's strength to stay clean in his weakness.

She needed space to consider this. In the end, Carmen chose to accept this cross of perseverance. Jesus helped her in solitude to release fear and rest in his control over the marriage. And quite unexpectedly, this strong and contained woman was able to reveal tenderly to Fernando how much she needed him, and how painful was the prospect of him choosing images of a woman over her. She wept. He held her. He assured her of his love and commitment to her. They confirmed how much they needed each other. And they both discovered in solitude new dimensions of the cross—God's power enabling them to go the distance as individuals on behalf of their marital union. Solitude helped them to sink into God, their Source, and so find new strength with which to love each other well.

MASTURBATION

Jake boldly questioned me about masturbation after one session. He admitted frankly that solitude was a struggle for him; aloneness amplified his sexual tension and often resulted in self-stimulation. Yes, he was overcoming porn addiction. Through hard, daily effort, he was refusing new and false images that fueled his struggle. But he still relied upon masturbation three or four times a week (it had been once or twice daily). He wanted to know if he was wrong to masturbate.

First, I encouraged his progress. He was adding no new wood to the fire, and the fire had lessened. I told him simply that my goal for anyone is progressive freedom from masturbation—to rely upon it less and less as one grows in Christ. And yes, I said, it is better to masturbate than to violate another human being through illicit sex. Yet, though it is the lesser of two evils, masturbation remains a violation of one's own "house."

Why a violation? Jake asked for a scripture reference. I had none, but pointed to God's bigger purposes for our sexuality. If the goal of our sexuality is to give ourselves away to others—to open the doors and windows of our house to others, to become known to and by them and maybe even at some point to break down a few walls and actually join with another—does masturbation serve that goal or hinder it?

Jake was unsure. At first he did not see how masturbation would hurt a relationship. I then asked him how he felt after he masturbated: free and ready for others, or uneasy, a little ashamed? He acknowledged some guilt. He thought about the wedge masturbation might actually create between himself and others. Could it inhibit genuine self-giving? Like John White says, "It frustrates the very instinct it gratifies."

I described my awareness of how deeply rooted that habit can be. Many people I know began to masturbate in childhood due to loneliness and the anxiety of living in some pretty painful situations. Self-stimulation helped ease the pain of real life.

Still others began to masturbate due to exposure to porn, sexual abuse and sex-play with other kids. Boundaries were broken early on, and the body responded. Over and over.

Undoubtedly, masturbation is a common thing. And it is also a childish thing. It does not encourage the kind of giving that adults want to offer other adults. Our own worlds of desire and release cannot satisfy our longing for real relationships. Maybe masturbation is better without fantasy, but that alone does not qualify it as something helpful. Maybe we all need to consider how we might lay aside the childish thing of masturbation.

Still, Jake could not imagine living without the sexual release masturbation afforded him. He admitted to me that his habit went back to childhood and intensified with porn and abuse. He struggled to believe that he could stop. I urged him to keep taking small steps toward relying less and less upon it. I invited him to lay claim to solitude as a potential garden, not the desert of moral failure. I helped him to think of his bed and bathroom (the sites of masturbation for him) as holy ground. He loved musical worship; I urged Jake to begin each day in worship: to offer his whole self to the Lord. I urged him when sexual feelings came up to offer those unto the Lord, not to suppress but to confess them and let them go. I reminded him of the dream he had some months before of a beautiful woman—lovely and appealing, yet pure, not a temptress.

That helped him to see that his sexual desires were not the enemy—he was actually overcoming the enemy's design for his sexuality. While the enemy wanted to stir up longings in Jake that were compulsive and demeaning and evil, God was intent on redeeming that desire. Easing his reliance upon masturbation helped redeem the good of that desire. God is intent on restoring our self-control so we can love others well.

Jake slowly made progress. He put forth the necessary effort.

He worshiped every morning, offering his whole self to the Lord. He took time each day—fifteen minutes eventually became thirty—just being still before the Lord: letting desires come up through the power of the cross and out upon the cross, receiving grace deeply, meditating on a few Scriptures, praying for loved ones.

As he used to masturbate in the shower, he covenanted with his roommate (with whom he shared the bathroom) if he might keep the bathroom door open during showering to inhibit that from happening. It seemed like a strange idea but it actually worked.

Solitude began to work peace in his soul that he hadn't known before. Being alone before God heightened sexual desire, but persevering through the tension eased that desire and granted peace to his soul. He discovered after a few weeks that he had more self-control. Still he battled.

The nights were hardest. Going to sleep was tough—the urge to masturbate intense. I urged him to try worship music as a way of focusing his thoughts before sleep. If that didn't work, to get up, pace the room prayerfully while extending his hands to God. Much of his sexual tension was bound up in pent-up physical tension, so I encouraged him to ensure a lot of exercise in this time.

He progressed and regressed and learned to be gracious with himself. His accountability partners prayed for him. He was beginning to open up to them at new levels; that too expended his energies in a positive way that helped him gain more self-control. Jake was learning: he could be alone with God and persevere in a good way with sexual desire until the longing for release passed. And while saying no to masturbation, he could say yes to what was good: sexual desire, the beauty and value of women, God's gracious presence, trustworthy friends, and his own dignity and value as a masculine being. That was easier to bless and value as he acquired self-control. He was becoming mature in his sexuality. Solitude was a part of that maturing.

FINDING HER OWN SONG

A big barrier to solitude for many, including Lucy and Rick, was the sheer amount of time they spent on virtual realities: instant messaging, e-mails, Facebook, downloading movies, music, and so on. Although both spent a lot of time alone, it was usually with some technical accompaniment. Both admitted that they struggled to be alone in the quiet of their own souls. That actually did make it hard for them to pray. Without a song or an image or a message to respond to, they didn't quite know what to do with themselves. They needed to deepen in quiet before the Lord.

Lucy enjoyed her aloneness. Probably a bit too much. When I inquired further it seemed like her solitude had a soundtrack, a steady stream of songs that her iPod fed her like an I.V. I asked her what she listened to. For as long as she could remember, she had sought refuge in sad or angry songs, written and sung mostly by women. In their voices, she found a voice; they supported Lucy in her pain. As a Christian, she found female singers who helped strengthen her hand in God. Most of them tended toward the "confessional" mode with a hint of melancholy. They met her in suffering but lifted her eyes to God. Not bad: one must go through Calvary to get to Pentecost, after all.

How did their voices impact her prayer life? She admitted that listening to music was her sole way for getting in touch with God. It was at once emotional and spiritual to her. I told her of my past tendency to worship and pray with music and how lost I was when my iPod broke. I no longer had any troubadours to take me to the throne room. It exposed my reliance upon another's response to God to get me in touch with mine. I then entered for the first time into extended periods with God alone—no other sound but my breathing and his Word and presence. I felt stripped. I no longer had another's divine romance to rely upon, and yet it was what God wanted to help me know what was in my heart and to offer that to him.

I urged Lucy to fast for a week or two from her endless stream of songs. She was a bright and articulate girl; I encouraged her that solitude might help her find her own voice of confession and devotion. That took longer than she liked. Like anyone unaccustomed to silence, she first became aware of the clutter in her heart. I encouraged her to sing a simple song of devotion: to honor him as she had through others' praise. Then to let secondary emotions and desires arise and release them without fuss, thus freeing her to focus on what was actually going on inside.

She made connections quickly and began to make her heart's condition and cry a big part of her prayer to God. Lucy loved to write and so she journaled much of this afterward. Things became clear to her. She became more aware of daily bruises and scrapes with others. Instead of distancing herself from them (a familiar pattern), she began to pray about the hurts, cry for justice and extend grace, and ask God to make her one who loves honestly and well—her eyes and heart open wide. She saw and felt things in solitude she missed while listening to another's story and worship.

I urged her to put the words into verse, even to try her hand at songwriting. She did, reluctantly at first. She came up to me after one session and recited some of the "first fruit" of her own story-telling. It was easy to encourage her song and the story it tells. Through solitude, Lucy is attending to that story and the song of gratitude that flows through it. God's mercy is growing in Lucy. She is learning to listen to her life and the still small voice speaking into it. New expressions of creativity are the fruit of Lucy's solitude.

FACEBOOK "FILLER"

I chatted with Rick about Facebook. He spent a lot of time posting pictures and updates and witnessing others do the same. He filled many empty hours doing so. I asked him why; he responded that it helped him feel connected with a lot of people. I asked him if it helped him deal with the conflict he was feeling in his immediate community (coming out of a troubled relationship, a recent rejection from a woman, etc.) He looked blank. He then admitted how Facebook helped him forget about it.

Fair enough. We all need diversions. But displacement does not resolve conflict; it just puts it off. I urged him to go on a Facebook fast for a week or so. Instead of logging on, I encouraged him to chose a few Scriptures and get alone with God. I also asked him to feel what came up in his heart in the quiet and to write those emotions and thoughts down.

He was wary about doing so ("I hate being alone!" he protested), but willing to try. The first session was terrible for him. His mind wandered all over and it seemed like a waste of time. He tried again, praying earnestly that God would meet him. He felt his brokenness—the loneliness and wounding that undergirded those failed relationships. He recited a few favorite Scriptures.

God's favor through Scripture countered his shame. Something happened. Like water priming a dry pump, he began to respond with weeping. These were tears of grief, and also gratitude. A greater love was wooing him and meeting him in solitude.

Other benefits: he came to a genuine personal remorse and anger at his perverse "mentor"; he felt guilt for his foolish zeal

in engaging with a sweet girl he was not ready to date. He felt
hatred for the man who rejected him due to his same-sex attraction. He hated all such men. He realized that he hated the
cruelty of those inclined to disdain homosexuality rather than
to show mercy. His heart was full of emotion and conflict.

Solitude urged him to recognize these conflicts in the light
of grace. I urged him to stay tuned through God's grace to the
real conflicts and relationships he was working out in his real
life. Solitude was a big part of that. Facebook, though fun and
chatty, is not the stuff of real community. God calls all of us to
work out complex relationships that cannot be posted in pictures and random observations. Knowing his heart and our
own in the complexity of our relationships requires solitude. It
prepares us for real community life.

SOLITUDE AND COMMUNITY

Bonhoeffer describes well the link between solitude and community:

> Let him who cannot be alone beware of community. He
> will only do harm to himself and to the community. Alone
> you stood before God when he called you; alone you had
> to answer that call; alone you had to struggle and pray;
> and alone you will die and give an account to God. . . . If
> you refuse to be alone, you are rejecting God's call to you,
> and you can have no part of the community of those who
> are called. . . . But the reverse also is true. Let him who is
> not in community beware of being alone. Into the com-
> munity you were called, the call was not meant for you
> alone; in the community you were called to bear your
> cross, you struggle, you pray. You are not alone, even in
> death, and on the Last Day you will be only one member

of the great congregation of Jesus Christ. . . . We recognize, then, that only as we are within fellowship can we be alone, and only he that is alone can live in fellowship.

Out of solitude, our friends began to see fruit in their lives together. All were less inclined to make others something they could not be. They were more apt to recognize and accept the limits of mere created beings. Sourced in the Creator, they ceased to demand that the creature satisfy all their needs.

A challenge to freedom in relationships is the confusing signals we give each other. Loving well requires clarifying those signals and setting boundaries. Sometimes solitude plays a key role here. Alone, emotions and desires surface that alert us to the need to clarify who one is to another, and who one is not.

Lucy suffered after the break-up of her most significant male relationship. God was faithful (as we have seen) to help her see it as a healthy and holy experience. Still, without him, she felt alone and tempted by despair. Another young man, a friend, cared for her in this time, and physically affirmed her through hugs, light backrubs, etc. She appreciated it but could see the danger in her feelings and in his friendly ignorance of the bond being formed.

In solitude, she became aware of sexual fantasies for this man whom she knew was a substitute for the love she had lost with another. It was unfair to both to continue in that way. Still, she did not want to lose a friend. She could readily affirm her gratitude for that friendship; it was harder to set a boundary with him physically, and to convey that such physical attention communicated a kind of love that he probably did not intend.

It was hard for Lucy to initiate that conversation. But solitude prepared her for it. When she was ready, she spoke the truth of her need for certain limits in the relationship. Her friend honored those limits, and actually respected her for making the hard effort to get out of the gray area both were relating in. Their brief talk invited him to look at his behaviors in a different way, and it freed them to have a supportive relationship without confusion. That boundary gave Lucy freedom to grieve a necessary loss and to clarify a friendship. In time, the desert of her aloneness became a garden. There is life after the death of a good relationship!

INSPIRED SELF-CONTROL

Sometimes solitude is the ground on which we work out self-control and thus prepare to be good gifts to each other. Such was the case for Jake. Solitude forced him to face his addiction to masturbation. He needed to learn how to restrain himself privately so that his "public" offering was free from shame and impurity.

That was (and is) a long, arduous process for him, as addicts are not inclined to solitude. But he is intent on turning the desert into a garden, one that is genuinely creative. I urged him onward in his quest for sobriety with the truth that I managed to forego masturbation for twelve months before marrying Annette. Not relying on masturbation helped prepare me for a real relationship, and it taught me that I could forego masturbation in the stress and pressure of married life.

In spite of the pleasures of marital sex, marriage alone will not spring the trap of masturbation. Quite the contrary: marriage can create tensions that may tempt one to self-stimulation. So it helps to lay aside masturbation before marriage, through the grace of God and good friends. Such self-control is a gift to one's spouse; it celebrates the other as one who is worthy of being loved sexually, rather than a means to the end of satisfying oneself. And it helps ensure that one can and will find healthy ways of coping with stress rather than masturbation.

Solitude prepares us to be a good offering to others. Sometimes our time alone with God frees us simply to savor others. We emerge out of solitude grateful and primed to speak words of blessing.

SOLITUDE AND GRATITUDE

I remember a tough season for Annette and me. We had been battered by a series of hardships; weary beyond words, we failed to draw from the well of each other. I took refuge for a few days of prayer and fasting in a desert monastery. It was winter—wind lashed the barren hills surrounding the place. As eating was the main source of fellowship at the monastery, I had nowhere to look for consolation but from God. His Word and presence fed me.

I had a lot of reflecting to do. In the quiet, I reckoned with the sting of loss and misplaced expectations. I felt them. I wondered where my heart was in it all: Had any vain or lustful thing been conceived? In the pain, had any created thing charmed me or threatened to become an idol? The waters of God's mercy rose as I kept myself fixed on him. I didn't strain; I just let the river accomplish what only it could: cleansing, delineating and healing. I gave to God my sin, the uncertainties of ongoing conflict that only he could oversee, and the weak places of my heart that invited holy strength.

All the while I longed for Annette. In the quiet, away from the din of ministry battles, my heart was filled with gratitude for her. I alighted upon memories of her goodness, her sorrow, her wisdom and her beauty in facing openly the tensions of the last few months. We had not been tested like this before. I had not seen her value as clearly as in those moments. I was filled with gratitude, holy love, for this amazing woman with whom

I had signed up for life. Passion welled up in my hungry, cold body. I was ready to come down the mountain and go home!

I realized afresh that solitude prepares me to be a more pure and sensitive offering to others, beginning with my wife. Solitude helps us to become truly creative in our relationships.

9

ZEAL FOR HIS HOUSE

BROKEN TO SERVE

You are no longer foreigners and aliens, but fellow citizens with God's people and members of God's household, built on the foundations of the apostles and prophets, with Christ Jesus himself as the chief cornerstone. In him the whole building is joined together and rises to become a holy temple in the Lord. And in him you too are being built together to become a dwelling in which God lives by his Spirit.

EPHESIANS 2:19-22

We have a building from God, an eternal house in heaven, not built by human hands. Meanwhile we groan, longing to be clothed with our heavenly dwelling . . . and would prefer to be away from the body and at home with the Lord. So we make it our goal to please him.

2 CORINTHIANS 5:1-2, 8-9

had been struggling with feelings of lust and depression on the eve of an international gathering of leaders. In the busyness and pressure, I was simply more vulnerable to my familiar "robbers." While cleaning house in preparation for the first round of guests, I looked with horror out the window: a four-foot black snake had slithered up from a crack in the foundation of the house onto the staircase of my back porch then landed on a large planter box just inches from the window! It was soon joined by another snake; the two dug a large hole where they began to mate.

Great, I thought, as I imagined hundreds of junior black snakes invading my house. I had to act. I went to get a shovel to kill them (sorry, this city boy didn't know better); I thought if my wife saw these monsters she would leave me and the house for her own sanity. (OK, we are both babies.) Shovel in hand, I looked out the window and noticed they were gone. Gone? In two minutes? I raced out onto the porch only to greet the snakes as they slithered right at me. I began to wildly swing the shovel at them and they raced off stunned but still slithering. I whacked them a few times while running after them, and they disappeared in the long grass, never to be seen again.

When I calmed down, I realized that this episode was important—not because the snakes posed a danger to anything but my naivety about snakes. Perhaps it was a prophetic picture of my "house" and its robbers. The snakes had found a place in the foundation of my house; they were familiar to me. And in truth some of the perverse sensual images I was seeing and subsequent sadness and heaviness I was feeling felt familiar—these are common temptations to me. I recalled the snakes mating, and I remembered how the spirit of impurity and despair go together—perversion begets death, death perversion, and so on.

The visual witness of the snakes mating woke me up. The Spirit arose in me and gave me zeal to protect my house by purging it of something evil that will multiply if I let it—if I accommodate the robbers. I had to act. I did. I made it clear to the snakes that they could not stay in my house anymore. The house belonged to my wife and me. There God has freed us to live in purity and creativity, with an expectancy of new life, not the dread of oppression.

God in his mercy freed me to see the danger and to battle accordingly. Otherwise, I would have stumbled through this international gathering preoccupied by robbers. Ashamed of my lust, depressed, I would have failed to represent Christ to the churches around the world represented in our gathering.

Every Christian has a similar responsibility—to know God's presence in his or her own "house" and to ensure that house stays clean and true to the One whose home it has become! His house refers to the body, or temple, of each one of us. That house also refers to the Body of Christ, or the corporate gathering of those who house Christ individually. The health of each believer's body depends significantly upon the wholeness of their relationship to the greater body.

That makes us subject to the church. And it is tough to stay clean and whole when the church surrounding us is unclean. Dirty leaven has power to sully the whole batch (1 Corinthians 5:6-7). Yet the healing that Christ imparts to us individually can influence the church powerfully. Rather than be conformed to the threat of "leaven," we can help transform her with the light and life we have received from Christ in his body. That's something I try to impart to any person troubled by a painful, unjust history with the church—you can make a difference.

Instead of approaching the church dreadfully, as one waiting to be victimized, I urge each one in the healing process to see the gift that they are to the church. In truth, that healing is community property. Though deeply personal, our healing possesses authority to release those we love out of the mercy and truth that has raised us from the dead.

That involves a zeal for something greater than simply one's own well-being; it involves grasping the heart of Jesus for his beautiful, being-restored temple. Scripture describes Jesus as an ardent bridegroom in love with his bride, the church. Surely he loves no one thing more passionately and zealously than his corporate "house," the church. Bound to him, we are thus bound to his ardor for his bride—our own temples and the greater temple they compose.

Scripture gives us no more passionate glimpse of this love than in Jesus' clearing of the temple.

Each Gospel describes his purge of the buyers and sellers there; Mark describes them as "robbers" (Mark 11:17) who were turning the house of Jesus' Father into a market (John 2:16). Zeal consumed him to expel thieves who profane the temple for their profit (Mark 11:17).

He is passionate in his refusal of such robbery. That house is for prayer, not commerce. He wants his people to commune intimately and powerfully in his Father's house, and manifest that communion in real love, not in selfish conniving or the greed that is idolatry. The only exchange he wants in the temple is human sin for divine mercy. Love casts out lust there; prayerful, humble communion prevails in the house Jesus indwells.

I thought poignantly of the attempted robbery of Carmen and Fernando's marriage; of Jake and the robbers of lust and control over women; of Bev and how her uncle stole her childhood; of Rick robbed of masculine security; of Lucy of her beauty and value as a woman. Gratefully, I also recalled God's faithful love to give them back double for all their sins. He is being glorified as the Lord and restorer of their temples.

A GIFT TO THE CHURCH

What has defined the restoration of each one is the local church. Each has found there "a church within a church" where they could be known in intimate areas of their lives. Wise mentors coupled with ongoing small group prayer and support made the difference. In truth, each has found a place for the great exchange: their sin and brokenness for divine truth and grace.

God was evident to them in his church, freeing each to become a good gift for others. He is glorified in their emergence as holy men and women—a people bearing Christ's name and his authority to love well—and each possesses power to discern and disarm intruders who seek to harass the temple. Each now lives according to the truth of his or her true self, one called to grow passionately in love with others, within the lines that dignify all involved. Each is becoming a witness to their surrounding community. Each seeks to live in the body honorably and well. That means clear, decisive action when necessary. He gives mercy when we humble ourselves before others and battle with his weapons.

We stand with Christ united in zeal for the dignity of our own houses. Then we can engage clearly and lovingly with others and so build up his greater house, the church. And it's a battle. We can learn to battle the right way and help make his house clean and strong.

I love Paul's words to the Corinthians when he said to them, "I am jealous for you with a godly jealousy. I promised you to one husband, to Christ, so that I might present you as a pure virgin to him. But I am afraid that just as Eve was deceived by the serpent's cunning, your minds may somehow be led astray from your sincere and pure devotion to Christ" (2 Corinthians 11:2-3). Virginal yet still subject to thoughts that derail sincere and pure devotion to Christ—that seems as relevant to our personal houses as well as to our beleaguered local churches. I feel Paul's godly jealousy for us all, that we might go the distance in sincere and pure devotion to Christ and each other. I pray that our legacy will be one of genuine devotion that engenders the same in our churches.

Virginal. Technically, we may not be physical virgins, but God can make our houses new by his blood and Spirit. Our grateful, undivided devotion to Jesus is what makes us truly virgin. We receive him as the One who makes all things new, beginning with ourselves and our broken histories. We resist false lovers for his name's sake; he gives his authority to do so. We then love him above all else. We agree with his Word that only in human marriage can we be naked and unashamed. In the meantime, we live as celibates, awaiting as earthy virgins his leading in human partnerships.

In that waiting period, we practice celibacy out of devotion to himself, the bridegroom King. We do so also out of our desire to love others well, without using sensuality to confuse or control others. I love how John Paul II speaks of virginity in regards to the church: "The Church is a virgin who keeps whole and pure the fidelity she has pledged to her Spouse." We as the house of Christ are to be virginal in our sincere and pure devotion to him and in how we care for each other. Each of us can commit ourselves to "virginal" living in preparation for what lies ahead for us relationally. We can ensure that Jesus is foundational to our relational future, whatever that might look like.

John Paul again writes: "Virginity is not restricted to a mere 'no' but contains a profound 'yes'" to Jesus and his order— "the gift of self for love" in its fullness. We must take that yes to Jesus seriously; we do so by heeding Paul's warning to the Corinthians that they could lose the virginity of their devotion to Jesus—pure and sincere—if they got entangled in sexual immorality.

WITNESS OF THE BODY

In 1 Corinthians 6, the apostle Paul declared powerfully that the human body belongs to the Lord; to him, the purity of the gospel is linked intrinsically to sexual purity. Jesus has made us his own—our bodily frames are intended for him. He has bought us with a price (his blood and cross), raised us with his power (filled with his Spirit) and destined us to be raised again in this very body on the last day.

To Paul, the whole gospel was at stake in how the Corinthians understood their bodies as earthy vessels of his holiness. He had made them virginal, and he wanted them to stay that way through living within the truth of his design for their sexuality. In the words of Christopher West, their bodies had theological meaning—what they did with their bodies testified to the God they served.

Paul in particular did not shy away from addressing the excesses at hand at Corinth, excesses that have marked Christians ever since. Lucy could have been one of the Corinthian women who wanted to live in the "not yet" of an entirely spiritualized existence. Her wounding from men was such that she wanted a desexualized world that particularly excluded broken men! Paul addressed error when he exhorted them: "In the Lord, however, woman is not independent of man, nor is man independent of woman. For as woman came from man, so also man is born of woman. But everything comes from God" (1 Corinthians 11:11-12).

Christian spirituality had not liberated Lucy from having to rely upon men rightfully; his grace freed her to do so, in fits and starts. Similarly, Jake, who best exemplified the addictive practices of the Corinthian men, had to bring his sensuality under the authority of Christ Jesus. Christ was freeing Jake to live with dignity in his body, and through progressive self-control, to begin to value women as worthy of his respect and restraint.

Being virginal is not a state of separation from the human body and its desires and needs; being virginal is about staying true to Christ in how one navigates those desires and needs. Fernando and Carmen were married and thus free for sexual love; they needed to heed Paul's words to not withhold the good gift of their sexual offering from one another (1 Corinthians 7:1-6).

The Corinthians lived in a world not unlike our own. The pagan culture surrounding them was so saturated with sex that Christian marrieds and singles alike were tempted to divorce their spirituality from their sexuality. Paul refuses. He anchors the human body squarely in Christ, and thus liberates the power of love to redeem the creativity of human sexuality, and restrain its cruelty.

What Paul refuses to do is make sex and marriage and family an idol, as if one's salvation hinged upon a blessed domestic partnership. He clearly reckons with the Christian's need to make peace with the other gender and to keep fire (sex) in the fireplace (heterosexual marriage). Yet he refuses to make relational bliss a goal. To the apostle, Christ is all; Christ is enough and should be the path and guide for the Christian in his or her relational pursuits. He blesses both marrieds and singles and refuses to decry the former as less spiritual. But he urges all Christians that the time is short, that the world as we know it is passing away quickly, and so we by inference labor in vain to emphasize too much the quality of our sexual and relational lives (1 Corinthians 7:29-31). His urgent word for all who aspire to God's best on earth? "Live in a right way in undivided devotion to the Lord" (1 Corinthians 7:35).

Paul wanted us to have zeal for the house of his Father. He wanted us to live virginally, in sincere and pure devotion to him and to reflect that in our relationships. But he would not have tolerated what can be a preoccupation with our relational quality of life. I refer here to what can be our consumer mentality toward relationships.

Many of us possess a sense of entitlement in which others must leap over a high threshold in order to satisfy our sophisticated "needs." Like relational gourmands, we wince at having to tolerate imperfection—the quirks and cracks in others and ourselves that guarantee flawed partnerships.

ACCEPTING AFFLICTION

The truth is, we all are subject to affliction—aches and pains tied to relational losses and sexual brokenness that may not entirely heal this side of heaven. Carmen had to refuse daily the fear that Fernando would choose impure images over her; Fernando had to choose daily not to do so. Bev lived within certain limits in relation to women to whom she felt attracted and sought the grace she needed to see men as potentially good gifts to her. Lucy forsook the lie daily that she was nothing without a man; she sought to live as a daughter of honor with or without a boyfriend. Rick still yearned at times for sensual images of manhood. He was learning to walk in the truth that he possessed all that he needed to be a whole-enough man without such images.

In light of the fragility we bear in these bodies, Paul implores us: live undivided lives in sincere and pure devotion to Jesus. Such devotion is the basis for forming life-giving relationships in Christ's Body. Undivided devotion to him helps us to develop whole relationships—though there are some qualifications. Wholeness can become an elusive "quality of life" term that applies only to those who have the time and money to aspire to such a privileged state.

I am aware that those who major on the healing of brokenness can unwittingly find themselves in a kind of therapeutic "prison." Through its bars, one may see and seek to include only those now deemed "whole-enough." Love is offered to the winsome creatures emerging out of the healing waters, while others are dismissed on the grounds that they are "toxic," unrealized. In that way, the pursuit of wholeness can become bondage; we may disqualify ourselves and others based on some rarified criteria that render us self-absorbed and selective in whom we deem worthy of love. Wisdom in our relationships is good, partiality isn't—James 2:1-13, for example.

Jesus wants us to see ourselves and others through the bars of the cross.

Paul claims that through the cross the world was crucified to him and he to it (Galatians 6:14). So too for us. Any worldly notions of "wholeness" need to be subordinated to the cross: we are crucified with Christ and raised up by powerful mercy to love others out of a sincere and pure devotion to him.

Perhaps that is in part what Paul intended when he warned the Corinthians not to aspire to relational heights at the expense of the gospel. "You were bought at a price; do not become slaves of men" (1 Corinthians 7:23). In other words, don't allow the traditions of mere men, relationally speaking, to siphon off your sincere and pure devotion to Jesus. That applies to those wanting to dissolve less than perfect marriages and to singles deceived by the lie that only marriage can complete their humanity.

Yes, we want the integrity of Christ's whole image. Yes, we

want to be faithful and want faithfulness from our intimates. No, we don't want to so analyze and scrutinize every flaw and flare-up of disorder that we fail to offer ourselves to God and others out of gratitude for his enormous mercy. In that way, the weaknesses that remain in ourselves and others have a certain visceral authority to draw us closer to the source of a pure and sincere devotion. And to free us to love others generously out of the enormity of God's grace toward us, a grace especially realized in our weakness.

Affliction can be a friend that draws us to Christ and his love. Receiving and extending that love is the only way to his power becoming mature in our weakness, whatever form that weakness may take on.

We wait in expectation. All of us live between the ages—the "now" of the body groaning, aching and only partially satisfied on earth, and the "not yet" of our ultimate release in full-bodied wholly spiritualized union with Christ. Christ's healing us on earth does not erase the ache; it simply liberates us to ache with a pure longing for Christ that shall never be sated this side of heaven.

GIFT OF CELIBACY

That is where the gift of celibacy is as important a witness on earth as marriage is. Abstinence applies to all as God calls all to learn to live within godly limits. That is as much a no to sexual immorality as it is a decisive yes to himself. God calls each one of us to spousal love and devotion—this is the gift of becoming "virgin" again. Out of a pure and sincere devotion to Christ, mercy makes us new daily, no matter how idolatrous one's history may have been.

Many will proceed on from there to discover partnership in marriage. But we err in assuming that marriage is the best solution for all. Far from a concession to our humanity, living a celibate life can be equally creative and rewarding to the married life. God has willed it so, and Scripture makes a strong case for the gift of celibacy. By that I am referring to Jesus' call to those who have renounced marriage for the sake of the kingdom of heaven (Matthew 19:12). Paul reinforces that call by describing celibacy as a gift that is desirable and achievable by virtue of the gift of God's grace (1 Corinthians 7:7).

Inspired celibacy bears witness on earth to a reality all Christians will encounter in heaven. That is, a heaven without marriage! In Matthew 22:30, Jesus claims that the glorified body will not be joined in marriage with another human. We will be joined with Christ. The inspired celibate on earth thus points to our heavenly future. John Paul II says it best: "Celibacy for the sake of the Kingdom of Heaven is a sign, a witness, a manifestation of the future time in which God will be everything to everyone."

Perhaps that informs a bit the grace God gives to celibates "to live in a right way in undivided devotion to the Lord" (1 Corinthians 7:35). That grace involves a life graced with the desire and discipline of pursuing intimate communion with the living God. Kierkegaard writes, "God wants celibacy because He wants to be loved. . . . I need something majestic to love . . . there was and still is in my soul a need for majesty, which I shall never grow tired of adoring."

Another mark of inspired celibacy is healthy self-giving. One does not cease to be a good gift to others as a result of abstaining from marriage—rather, they offer themselves all the more to others as a way of truly engendering new life in others, for the sake of the kingdom of heaven. That means rightful and intimate (within limits) partnership with others who are called to do the same.

I have witnessed remarkable fruitfulness with those who have settled their singleness before God and others. One of my best friends, Jonathan Hunter, embarked on a four-year exploration to discover whether or not God had given him the gift of celibacy. We who surrounded him in the community bore witness of the grace God was giving him to deepen in consistent intimacy with himself. Jonathan was also bearing fruit in ministry, employing his uninterrupted hours profitably for the kingdom.

Jonathan also chose to submit aspects of his latent sexuality—its emotional needs and sexual longings—to trusted friends like me. In his need for others and the occasional misdirected desire, Jonathan worked out his sexuality with integrity. That is another mark of a celibate gift—working out abstinence in truth and grace. God had given that gift to Jonathan; it was obvious to us all. At the right time, we soberly and joyfully laid hands on him and conferred the gift God had given Jonathan.

Another scenario may be helpful here. Many singles I know would like to be married but often wonder whether or not that will happen. As time passes, they consider their future on earth and realize it may not include marital partnership. Though currently celibate, they avoid describing themselves as "celibate." Their desire is marriage, not the celibate "gift." Time is making some reconsider if God has in truth gifted them to live inspired single lives for the sake of the kingdom.

One woman I know is an amazing healer and leader. She is beautiful—an extraordinary gift to all who know her. She has a great set of friends. She is at times lonely and worried about her future as a single woman. A non-Christian man began to gather with her set of friends and pay attention to her. She loved it. He tolerated her faith but would not embrace it. She began to weigh whether or not she could live in "sincere and pure devotion to Christ" joined with this fine pagan.

Her loneliness almost overtook her discernment. She found herself willing to leap over her understanding of truth (the folly of being "yoked with an unbeliever"; 2 Corinthians 6:14) in order to secure her future. She wrestled with her decision. She was shocked by her openness to forsaking the truth. Then she thought of the community she had found in Christ—the deep and trustworthy and altogether fruitful bonds she had forged in his Body. Was she willing to lose that for a mere man?

Having been bought with a price, she ran the risk of becoming enslaved to men (1 Corinthians 7:23). She gratefully and quickly came to her senses. She wanted Christ. She wanted pure devotion. She wanted fruitfulness based on the covenant she had made with Christ through his Body. God showed her the heart of the matter: "pure and sincere devotion," to himself and the community she loves. It was a no-brainer for her to redraw the broken lines with that man in order to solidify a friendship and exclude him as a prospective spouse.

She has a spouse. Jesus truly is the lover of her soul. Is she now a resolute celibate for the rest of her days on earth? She hopes not. She hopes for a lover in the flesh. But she now spells that "hope" with a lowercase *h;* marriage is no longer her most urgent need. Devotion to Jesus is. Like the psalmist, she realizes that her days are numbered; in that she is learning wisdom (Psalm 90:12). Her life is but a shadow of the glorious union yet to come when she sees Jesus face to face. He has become her hope.

So we put Christ first, and demonstrate that hope by how we care for each other—seeking to be good gifts and receiving what others can and will give us. In that, we grow in love, with Christ our solid foundation. And we help one another prepare for the real deal—eternity.

Whether single or married, we help each other prepare for

the ultimate spousal reality—the resurrection of the body in union with Christ. That is our bodily resurrection from the dead and the "the life everlasting" that Paul spends a lot time reminding us about (1 Corinthians 15). We await the body's ultimate and everlasting purpose: intimacy with Jesus Christ. We thus help each other now to steward gracefully the ignoble groaning and hiccups of our bodies on earth. We do so in preparation for its glorious future, the body raised in power and in the image of the risen Christ (1 Corinthians 15:42-49).

NEEDING THE CHURCH

For that, we need the greater body. To prepare individual bodies for him, we need the Body of Christ. We need to maintain zeal for that greater Body, in order to prepare to see him face-to-face. For that, we need churches that value sorting out sexual and relational issues. Not all value that kind of ongoing, pastoral care in which we can freely share our afflictions with each other so that Christ may rest upon us. Rick said it best about the community he grew up in: "My church was excellent at introducing many to the Savior then at shaming them afterward for still needing that Savior!"

So what are some of the hallmarks of such a community?

Heart of the pastor. A key factor in introducing good solid pastoral care in the local church is the pastor's humble reckoning with the deep needs of his congregants. In truth, he or she tends a host of beautiful, gifted and really broken people. Every seeker of Jesus possesses good gifts to extend to others; each also needs space and grace to sort out barriers to extending and receiving those gifts. We are normal; we are broken. A good pastor knows this about his sheep and humbly makes a way for them to discover that Jesus wants to be Lord and healer of every aspect of one's life.

A humble pastor also realizes that he cannot do it all, especially in areas of sexual and relational redemption. It requires
too much effort for any one person to take on that task. So the
pastor must be humble and wise enough to equip the saints
under his charge to do the work of this ministry (Ephesians
4:12). Solid parachurch ministries exist that can come alongside a pastor to help him equip lay persons to heal others in the
context of the church.

Integrity and boundaries. The best way forward is small
groups led by lay people, like Living Waters. What keeps these
groups safe is the integrity of the leadership. That means that
leaders are accountable to the elders in areas of weakness. In
other words, these leaders and groups have good boundaries.
What makes these groups safe for all concerned is the high
value placed on confidentiality. What goes on in the group stays
in the group. All involved are trained from the start that any
sharing about others in the group violates the essence of the
gathering and can be grounds for removal from the group.

The freedom to share about the deep realities tied to sexuality and relationships requires nothing less. If the Body is going
to free us to prepare our bodies for the Lord, we need to know
our secrets are safe. Relational integrity is built on trust. Securing that trust is key to the truth-telling and grace-giving that
sets us free to rightfully rely upon others in profound areas of
our lives.

Healing groups for sexual and relational redemption function as a safe and protected "church" within the greater church.
There one knows it is wise and possible to open up about areas
that would be foolish to reveal in, say, a home Bible study where
members gather to learn Scripture, not to probe the depths of
their inner humanity.

We subject ourselves and others to unnecessary risk when

we don't assess the proper context for opening up our sexual and relational issues to others. Still, such a context can be formed and protected by the boundary of keeping confidences. Then one can dare to be candid and begin to grow in the trust that truly is the basis for our freedom to love others. All of our friends directly linked the freedom to be honest with their church with the trust they ascribed to the group itself and its boundaries. That takes church leaders who believe in Christ's Body as the place where such disclosure can and should occur.

Humble churches that heal. Many are finding refuge in churches where healing and discipleship in the sexual area is highly valued. Jake, Bev, Lucy, Rick, and Fernando and Carmen are walking in freedom today because they found such churches. Such an offering requires a humble church. In that way, the church that offers sexual redemption refuses the pride of the Laodiceans. God challenged them in Revelation 3:17: "You say, 'I am rich, I have acquired wealth and do not need a thing.' But you do not realize that you are wretched, pitiful, poor, blind and naked."

The Corinthians had a similar problem. They tended to congregate (and congratulate themselves) on the basis of their wisdom, affluence and advanced spirituality. As a result, they did not prefer people who could not measure up to their social and spiritual savoir faire. They did not highly value disclosing their "need," let alone their brokenness!

Paul really did not like that. He admonished them not to "despise the church of God by humiliating those who had nothing" (1 Corinthians 11:22). He implored them to "examine themselves" before taking communion together as a church in order to not take the meal unworthily (1 Corinthians 11:28). In context, the unworthy were not the obviously immoral but those who rejected joining with others based on a kind of spiritual pride and elitism.

Churches that possess zeal for working out deep issues together acknowledge how much they are the beautiful broken bride. And, in turn, how much they still need Jesus! They are neither afraid to say so nor afraid to provide the care that reveals this truth: the broken are among us.

I recall the roots of my early church experience and with gratitude see how many throughout the world are experiencing the same reality. As they persevere in the church, receiving the healing they need, they are changing the face of the church in their nations. They are revealing the face of Jesus who grants grace and space for his people to discover sexual redemption. Not in spite of his Body, but in it.

UNITY IN DIFFERENCE

When I first committed myself to a local church, I discovered very few who shared my homosexual struggle. But many freely acknowledged the challenge of living purely in the idolatrous heterosexual world around them. These ones gave me access to their devout lives. However weak they may have been, they were stronger than I in Christ. Through them I received power to persevere and a vision for a better way to commune with others. I also discovered that our sharing worked both ways. My presence in the lives of those who were, in truth, more whole actually invited a few of them to look at the brokenness underneath their wholeness.

One man quietly disclosed to me that his marital sex life was in shambles due to the guilt both he and his wife felt over sex they shared before marriage. A woman who led worship for the church disclosed her quiet, unrealized same-sex attraction; another man, a psychiatrist, confessed his struggle to stay clean with his new girlfriend. I began to see that my desire to bring healing to homosexuals could possibly include a good percentage of the church!

What was happening was clear—I the weaker was submitting to new friends and was getting stronger as a result! I also discovered that my being-healed life had meaning to their more apparently whole lives. That truth fulfilled Paul's words about diversity and unity in the church when he said to the Corinthians:

> The eye cannot say to the hand, "I don't need you!" And the head cannot say to the feet, "I don't need you!" On the contrary, those parts of the body that seem to be weaker are indispensable, and the parts that we think are less honorable we treat with special honor. And the parts that are unpresentable are treated with special modesty, while our presentable parts need no special treatment. But God has combined the members of the body and has given greater honor to the parts that lacked it, so that there should be no division in the body, but that its parts should have equal concern for each other. (1 Corinthians 12:21-25)

Here Paul mandates a rule of love expressed in mutual submission between different parts—the apparently lovely parts need the weaker and less honored parts, and vice versa. What might those body parts be: the "unpresentable" and less honored parts, as well as the indispensable "weaker parts"?

My interpretation has been forged in the trenches of churches where the likes of Carmen and Fernando, Rick and Lucy, Bev and Jake are working out their sexual and relational lives. They qualify for these categories; each can attest to the difficulty in presenting to others the shameful, hidden areas. And they can certainly testify to the weakness they often feel in making known to others what God has done and is still doing in their lives.

Commentators tend to agree that the "unpresentable" parts refer to human sexuality, the parts of the body that need to be treated with special modesty. They need to be "covered" by those parts that are rightfully, shamelessly outward and in full view. I see this as the way that God orders the Body in order to "cover" us in our unseen areas (wisely, I hope). In so doing, we have discovered trustworthy walking partners who help us to make the great exchange of damage and doubt for healing and personal clarity; these trusted ones then stand with us as we seek to walk out that exchange in our relationships. Those helpers define well the "covering" of the otherwise "unpresentable" parts. These blessed ones "give greater honor to the parts that lacked it." We receive healing and the dignifying of our humanity. The Body functions as God wills it to function—covering those in need—leaving little room for the division and impurity inspired by unattended sexual brokenness.

How many of us have been slammed in the Body by sexual sin? How many churches have been ravaged by adultery, the surfacing of sexual addictions, the "coming out" of yet another Christian leader? How much better to extend honor to those seeking it in their depths, and so ward off the "snakes" of sexual immorality?

Clearly that would benefit "the parts that lack honor." But it also applies to "the sleek and the strong." The "unpresentable ones" alert those seemingly in order and in control to the truth that they are not exempt from the idolatry of the age. Paul is clear: "So if you think you are standing firm, be careful that you don't fall! . . . And God is faithful; he will not let you be tempted beyond what you can bear. But when you are tempted, he will also provide a way out so that you can stand up under it" (1 Corinthians 10:12-13).

That means that even the most "presentable one" may be vulnerable. That has something to do with being a flawed human being. It also has something to do with an idolatrous culture: like Corinth, modern-day consumers worship sensual gods and goddesses.

Also, we will tend to be ensnared in areas of our lives that we have not disclosed to others. Precisely the depth and hiddenness of sexuality inclines the seemingly "whole" to temptation. Without Christ's Body as a preventative strike against sexual sin, we all can be vulnerable to it.

The candor of the unpresentables, now covered, makes a way for all to come clean. How marvelous this is. The fallen, now raised, have a unique authority to inspire holy prevention—"the way out" promised by Paul. Yes, their stories may at times contain exotic elements uncommon to most, but the depth and length of God's faithfulness to and through them invites all to face wisely the normal temptations common to humanity.

That is important. Remember, Paul wrote to the Corinthians that their wrong approach to the body and sex actually diminished their grasp of the gospel. Illicit sexual activities (and the arrogance that undergirded it) threatened the very gospel in their midst. God, through the apostle Paul, was intent on redressing the simple saving work of Christ as applied directly to their sexual and relational selves.

The gospel clearly has power to inspire right sexual ethics; purity and clarity of human relating in turn has power to make that gospel known. Paul wanted the body reclaimed for Christ. He wanted the greater "Body" to exercise its rightful authority toward that end. This to me is the power of the unpresentables; once covered by the Body, they have authority to invite others into his way for the body.

An example of Rick's influence might illustrate the point. As a healing lay leader in his church, he has a reputation for being "enthusiastic" about the power of Jesus to reclaim the body through the Body. Some of his friends appreciate it; others don't get it or find his passion irrelevant to their normal lives and mildly annoying.

Rick noticed that two of his rather annoyed friends (both married but not to one another) were paying an unusual amount of attention to each other. He knew the dance; it was only too familiar to him. He prayed and waited for the time to make known his concern. His discernment was correct: the two were falling in love and flirting with physical sexual immorality. They were in deception—blind to the illicit emotional bond and tempted strongly to break covenant with their families.

In highlighting what he saw at play, Rick invited them to "find the way out" before it was too late. They hated him for it and still have not fully accepted his role as a watchman. But each party heeded his warning and began to submit their unpresentable parts to those who could help them. They realized that they had to set new boundaries and begin to work on their respective marriages. Both unions are gratefully intact, the boundaries still in place. Rick discovered in those encounters that he had authority to help the "presentable ones" find a way of escape for their temptations.

Paul also refers to a second body part in 1 Corinthians 12—besides the unpresentable parts, he refers to the part that seems weaker but is indispensable to the whole (1 Corinthians 12:22). Commentators usually refer to this as an unseen internal organ. Though there are of course many internal organs, I want to refer to one in particular which healers in the areas of sexual redemption become for their local churches.

We function as the "liver" in Christ's Body. As we have discovered his mercy and truth in their unpresentable areas, we invite others into the purifying flood. It is a humble and little seen role. Many know nothing about it and when they do, readily avoid it. But what a function. How glorious the exchange of shame and fear and doubt and compulsion for dignity, confidence, clarity and the freedom to choose well in our human relationships.

They have discovered this exchange in their lives; now they have power to give it. Behind closed doors, with boundaries strong enough to protect the dignity of all involved, the power of Christ's blood finds its rightful aim. It breaks the power of real sin in real lives, and frees men and women to resume the good, hard task of loving each other well.

The operation of the liver cannot be downplayed. Think of the promise of the end: Jesus is returning for "a bride that has made herself ready. Fine linen, bright and clean was given her to wear" (Revelation 19:7-8). "She" is the church as clean in her "unpresentable" parts as she is in her outward displays. She will be (in truth, must be) a Body that has lived out her "sincere and pure devotion to Christ." Christ is returning for a virgin bride. Toward that end, Jesus activates the liver: quiet, little seen, yet indispensable to preparing the Body for its Head, the Bride for its Bridegroom.

Perhaps the biggest threat to her integrity is not the obviously broken ones but those who out of religious pride and duty claim to be ready and are not. In a time when the world and the worldly church is every bit as idolatrous as she was at Corinth, we need to hear the words of Jesus:

> You do not realize that you are wretched, pitiful, poor, blind and naked. I counsel you to buy from me gold refined in the fire, so you can become rich; and white clothes to wear, so you can cover your shameful nakedness; and salve to put on your eyes, so you can see. (Revelation 3:17-18)

How blessed are we who through our own "cross-walk" help reveal her need, and who then become a part of covering those in need. Stirring in our hearts is a zeal for his house, a zeal established in the work of holiness and healing he has wrought in us.

May we all be ready on the day of his return. In the meantime, may zeal consume us as we prepare a house worthy of Jesus.

The builder of a house has greater honor than the house itself. . . . And we are his house if we hold on to the courage and the hope of which we boast. (Hebrews 3:3, 6)

Hallelujah! For our Lord God Almighty reigns.
Let us rejoice and be glad and give him glory!
For the wedding of the Lamb has come,
And the bride has made herself ready. Fine linen bright and clean, was given her to wear.
[Fine linen stands for the righteous acts of the saints.]
(Revelation 19:6-8)

ACKNOWLEDGMENTS

Special thanks to Mike Nobrega and Morgan Davis, whose friendship is daily bread to me, and who helped me to steer clear of lesser meals while writing this book.

Without a pastor like Lloyd Rindels, I would not have had rich church soil in which to serve fellow strugglers while writing and so authenticate the book's theme and my boast—the local church is the best venue for healing the sexually broken.

And to my editor, Cindy Bunch; without your vision for this work, conveyed with clarity and kindness, the book would not have happened. You make me a better writer.

NOTES

Chapter 3: Laying a Sure Foundation

p. 49   needs for attention and affirmation and affection: Toni Dolfo-Smith, "Appendix 2: Understanding Our Need," in Andrew Comiskey, *Living Waters: Pursuing Sexual and Relational Wholeness in Christ* (Grandview, Mo.: Desert Stream Press, 2007), pp. 255-59.

pp. 50-51 "At some point in our lives": Ibid., p. 256.

p. 55   "So that love might be as great as possible": Simone Weil, "Waiting for God," in *Bread and Wine: Readings for Lent and Easter* (Farmington, Penn.: Plough Publishing, 2003), pp. 213-16. Reprinted from Simone Weil, "The Love of God and Affliction," in *Waiting for God*, trans. Emma Craufurd (New York: G. P. Putnam's Sons, 1979).

Chapter 4: Opening Doors

p. 65   "the deepest and most real possibilities and dispositions of our humanity": John Paul II, *The Theology of the Body: Human Love in the Divine Plan* (Boston: Pauline, 1997), p. 176.

p. 67   "The whole story of our salvation is contained": Christopher West, *The Love That Satisfies: Reflections on Eros and Agape* (West Chester, Penn.: Ascension, 2007), p. 12.

p. 69   "Our natural tendency is to treat people": Mike Mason, *The Mystery of Marriage*, Twentieth Anniversary Edition (Sisters, Ore.: Multnomah, 2005), pp. 45, 43.

p. 69   "Both deal in the most direct way possible": Ibid., p. 50.

p. 71   West refers to these two extremes as angelism or animalism: West, *Love That Satisfies*, p. 43.

p. 73   "Living with such beauty and blemish": Amy Mark Hall, *Kierkegaard and the Treachery of Love* (Cambridge: Cambridge University Press, 2002), p. 106.

p. 74   as God's image-bearers are unique in our capacity: Karol Wojtyla, *Love and Responsibility* (San Francisco: Ignatius, 1993), p. 41.

p. 77   "The correct gravitational pull that enables sentiment": West, *Love That Satisfies*, p. 142.

p. 77   "The command to love forces one to see the other": Hall, *Kierkegaard and the Treachery of Love*, p. 101.

p. 78   "Love is put to the test when the sensual and emotional attractions weaken": Wojtyla, *Love and Responsibility*, p. 134.

p. 81   "Love demands of each individual Christian": Hall, *Kierkegaard and the Treachery of Love*, p. 24.

p. 82   "is our only possible source of hope": Ibid., p. 103.

p. 83   "It is all love and love": Kierkegaard, quoted in ibid., p. 11.

Chapter 5: Housing Desire

p. 90   "knowing only Christ, and no longer oneself": Dietrich Bonhoeffer, "Discipleship at the Cross," in *Bread and Wine: Readings for Lent and Easter* (Farmington, Penn.: Plough Publishing, 2003), pp. 49-50. Reprinted from Dietrich Bonhoeffer, *Meditations on the Cross*, trans. Douglas W. Stott (Louisville: Westminster John Knox Press, 1998).

p. 91   "It is not our business to decide": Ibid., p. 27.

p. 91   "Am I willing to relinquish my hold": Oswald Chambers, *My Utmost for His Highest* (Grand Rapids: Discovery House, 1992), March 8: "The Surrendered Life."

pp. 92-93   "The imperative need spiritually is to sign": Ibid., March 21: "Interest or Identification."

p. 95   "Discernment requires, from the onset, one's consistent tendency toward self-deception": Amy Mark Hall, *Kierkegaard and the Treachery of Love* (Cambridge: Cambridge University Press, 2002), p. 60.

Chapter 6: Cleaning House

p. 117   I read an article: Author Unknown, "Obscene Losses," *Conde Nas Portfolio.*

p. 124   "Never before has so much obscenity been available": US Department of Justice, Post Hearing Memorandum of Points and Authorities, *ACLU v. Reno,* 929 F. Supp. 824 (1996).

p. 124   "Constant exposure to beautiful women has made single men less interested": J. P. Moreland, *Kingdom Triangle* (Grand Rapids: Zondervan, 2007), p. 104.

p. 124   We get fired up by some hipster's rendering: The Associated Press, "Dirty Song Lyrics Can Prompt Early Teen Sex," msnbc .com, August 7, 2006.

p. 124   Your average college student had ten partners: Daniel McGinn, "Mating Behavior 101," *Newsweek,* October 4, 2004.

p. 124   The first national study on sex and female teens: Lawrence K. Altman, "Sex Infections Found in Quarter of Teen Girls," *New York Times,* March 12, 2008, p. A1.

pp. 124-25 "Hook-ups do satisfy biology": quoted in Moreland, *Kingdom Triangle,* p. 28.

p. 125   "Although sex consummates the friendship of husband and wife": J. Budziszewski, *What We Can't Not Know* (Dallas: Spence, 2003), p. 100.

p. 125   A *Newsweek* cover story claims: David J. Jefferson, "The Divorce Generation Grows Up," *Newsweek,* April 21, 2008, pp. 48-53.

p. 126   Thomas Schmidt prophesied that homosexuality stood in the frontlines: Thomas Schmidt, *Straight and Narrow?* (Downers Grove, Ill.: InterVarsity Press, 1995), p. 11.

p. 127   HBO represented gay and bisexual characters in 42 percent: Dave Itzoff, "Study Rates Inclusion of Gay TV Characters," *New York Times,* July 27, 2009, p. C2.

p. 127   Researchers cite the new freedom young men and women have: John Cloud, "The Battle Over Gay Teens," *Time,* October 10, 2005, pp. 43-51.

p. 130   "I can now maintain hundreds of friendships": Christine Rosen, "Virtual Friendship and the New Narcissism," *The New Atlantis* 17 (Summer 2007): 15-31.

p. 130   "to have short-lived relationships marked by infidelity": The

Associated Press, "Narcissism on the Rise," *Kansas City Star*, February 26, 2007.

pp. 130-31   "Perhaps the most enduring failure of love today": Sister Wendy Beckett, *Love: Meditations on Love* (New York: DK Publishing, 1995), p. 27.

Chapter 7: Whole Houses

p. 142   "We must differentiate between the self that collaborates": Leanne Payne, *Restoring the Christian Soul* (Westchester, Ill.: Crossway, 1991), p. 26.

p. 162   "When you feel your heart sinking under trouble": François Fénelon, *The Royal Way of the Cross*, ed. Hal M. Helms (Brewster, Mass.: Paraclete, 1982), p. 143.

Chapter 8: Home Alone

p. 166   "Every one of us—not just those who are the most visibly wounded": Leanne Payne, *Listening Prayer* (Grand Rapids: Baker, 1994), p. 169.

p. 167   "Without solitude, we begin to cling to each other": Henri J. M. Nouwen, *Clowning in Rome* (Westminster, Md.: Christian Classics, 1992), pp. 15-16.

p. 169   "When people tell me they have trouble taking time for prayer": Gerald G. May, *The Awakened Heart* (New York: HarperCollins, 1993), p. 99.

pp. 170-71   "the lips and mind both come to rest": Jim Borst, *Coming to God* (Surrey, U.K.: Eagle, 1992), pp. 47-48.

p. 174   See through my eyes the one who wounded you: Retold from Andrew Comiskey, *Living Waters: Pursuing Sexual and Relational Wholeness in Christ* (Grandview, Mo.: Desert Stream Press, 2007), pp. 142-43.

p. 176-77   "Perseverance, translated literally, means: remaining underneath": Dietrich Bonhoeffer, *A Testament to Freedom*, ed. Geffrey B. Kelly and E. Burton Nelson (San Francisco: HarperSanFrancisco, 1995), p. 291.

p. 178   "it frustrates the very instinct it gratifies": John White, *Eros Defiled* (Downers Grove, Ill.: InterVarsity Press, 1977), p. 45.

pp. 184-85   "Let him who cannot be alone beware of community": Dietrich

Bonhoeffer, *Life Together* (Minneapolis: Augsburg Fortress, 2004), p. 82.

Chapter 9: Zeal for His House

p. 194   "The Church is a virgin who keeps whole and pure": John Paul II, *The Theology of the Body: Human Love in the Divine Plan* (Boston: Pauline, 1997), p. 475.

p. 194   "Virginity is not restricted to a mere 'no'": Ibid., p. 475.

p. 195   their bodies had theological meaning: Christopher West, *The Love That Satisfies: Reflections on Eros and Agape* (West Chester, Penn.: Ascension, 2007), p. 13.

p. 200   "Celibacy for the sake of the Kingdom of Heaven's sake is a sign": John Paul II, *Theology of the Body*, p. 267.

p. 200   "God wants celibacy because He wants to be loved": Kierkegaard as quoted by Raniero Cantalamessa, *Virginity: A Positive Approach to Celibacy for the Sake of the Kingdom of Heaven* (Staten Island, N.Y.: Alba House, 1995), p. v.

DESERT **STREAM**™
MINISTRIES

For more information on healing and equipping the sexually and relationally broken through the local church, please visit the Desert Stream Ministries website at <www.desertstream.org>.